Daily Acts:
Daily Holidays

For Group Settings
or a Stricter Budget

One Act at a Time Books, LLC

Authors: Savania North
        One Act at a Time Books, LLC
Illustrator: Catherine Highton

Choose to do activities based upon what is best for you. If you need to consult a parent/guardian, doctor or other professional before engaging in an activity, please, do so. Take any precautions you believe wise or necessary. Neither One Act at a Time Books, LLC nor the author assume any responsibility for the decisions you make or the results of those decisions. Various random sources were used to find holidays for each day, and were not verified to determine if they are in any capacity "official." In some instances, the author may have added or subtracted to the day. This is for fun while growing personally and contributing to the world around us, not the accuracy of the title or day.

To all the people who love God and want to make the world a better place.

and

To Grandma's sunshine. I hope we can help make the world a better place for you all.

CONTENTS

INTRODUCTION

Ever since I heard of them, I liked the concept of there being holidays for practically everything. Official national holidays are fine, but there is a day, week, or month to honor almost anything, from the fun, such as World Circus Day to the serious and moral, such as International Speak Out Month. As a Christian, I have wanted to find a way to turn these fun and interesting days into Christian acts of kindness and/or personal growth. My goal with this project is to complete at least one Christian act of kindness or personal growth for each day of the year, and I encourage others to do the same. After each day, I will leave spaces for you to write down your thoughts and experiences.

There are many holidays on lots of the days. I just chose one for each day, unless they could somehow blend together. Also, some days may be off a day or so as the years change. It personally does not bother me to complete an activity for an obscure holiday on the wrong day, but you can adjust accordingly if it is important to be on the correct day.

Before you begin, it would be wonderful if you would keep a Bible with this book, so you can refer to them together daily. A Bible passage reference is attached to each day, as is a suggested activity. Some of the same verses will be used for multiple days, when appropriate. This helps those verses to become more familiar, and easier to recall when needed in daily life situations.

You will notice that I include the Bible reference, and not the passage itself. This should make it more meaningful to you, and easier to remember and refer to when applicable real life situations occur. In using your own Bible, you choose the version of the Bible that you believe is most accurate and/or the easiest for you to understand. If this is your first time reading the Bible and/or you have difficulty in understanding it, you may want to start with a Bible that is in easier-to-understand language, with the knowledge that some accuracy may be lost, and then after you are more familiar with the Bible, change to one that you believe to be the most accurate direct interpretation of the original. I used a King James Version writing this book. You may also want a concordance, expository dictionary, or refer to commentaries, but that is entirely optional. Those resources are also easily available online.

Start at any point in the year, and when you get to the end of the book, jump back to the beginning until you, personally, have gone full circle. Then, go to the Reflections chapter to reflect on your journey and where you want it to lead next.

This book is not meant to just read, but to actively participate in daily activities, and record your experiences. Let my activity suggestions just be a consideration, something to start you thinking. You may choose similarly to what I suggest, something completely different, or anywhere in between. Just choose something that makes the day meaningful.

I am writing this during a pandemic. Situations like this may alter your choice of activities. Be creative and flexible with your choices.

Every act does not need to be something big or cost money. We are potentially doing something every day, so it would get expensive fast if we spent money each time. I do encourage that you reach out to people outside of your family often. Some activities may be for personal growth, or to benefit your family, but try to make sure that some reach out to the community as well.

This version of Daily Acts: Daily Holidays was developed for people in group settings. This could be church groups, small groups, groups in facilities such as nursing homes or prisons, or any type of group setting. It could also work well for individuals in these facility settings that are not necessarily working on this in a group, but individually. That is because this edition varies from the original in that the activities suggesting monetary donations are eliminated, and those having to do with food or outings are greatly reduced. Because of these changes, this version may also be best suited to people who are not in facility settings but have a stricter budget or limited resources and opportunities to do some of the activities in the original book.

If you are working on this individually, you will just want to write down your thoughts instead of 'discussing with the group', and may need to adjust some of the activities accordingly.

If you are a group leader, you may want to include in your notes what went well in the group and what did not, so that you will know how you may want to handle that activity next time. If you are the only member with a copy of the book, it would also be helpful if each member had a notebook to write down their thoughts for each day. You may also wish to encourage same day or next day discussions on activities that members

3

carried out individually. Determine what is best for the members and the situation that you have, and be sure to encourage members to only do what they can safely do, and to get medical or other professional advice before engaging in activities that could be of a concern to them.

January 1
Ellis Island Day-

The Bible passage I chose for today is Hebrews 12:14-15. Please, look it up and read it aloud to the group.

Discuss how this Bible passage relates to today's holiday.

Activity Suggestions:
1) Try a food from another culture that you have never had before.
2) Learn a fun fact about another country.
3) Learn how to say hello and goodbye in a new language. It does not have to be from another country. Sign language counts, too.
4) Listen to music from another country or culture. Make sure that the lyrics are appropriate and free of profanity.

What did you do today to observe this holiday? Add any thoughts about your experience.

January 2
National Motivation and Inspiration Day-

The Bible passage I chose for today is
Colossians 3:23. Please, look it up and read it aloud
to the group.

Discuss how this Bible passage relates to today's
holiday.

Activity Suggestion:
1) Write out all of your goals. Then, beside each
goal, write who and what motivates and inspires
you towards each goal. If you are lacking in
motivation and inspiration in any areas, what can
you do about that? One thing you could do is pray
about it, and God can give you those things.

What did you do today to observe this holiday?
Add any thoughts about your experience.

January 3
Celebration of Life Week-

The Bible passage I chose for today is
Psalm 16:11. Please, look it up and read it aloud to
the group.

Discuss how this Bible passage relates to today's
holiday.

Activity Suggestions:
1) Be aware of all the little pleasures in the day.
Write them down or comment on them. Do not
just overlook them and take them for granted.
2) Make a list of 20 things for which you are
grateful today.

What did you do today to observe this holiday?
Add any thoughts about your experience.

January 4
National Be On Purpose Month-

The Bible passage I chose for today is
James 1:19-20. Please, look it up and read it aloud
to the group.

Discuss how this Bible passage relates to today's
holiday.

Activity Suggestion:
1) Be intentional in what you say and do. Do not
just react. Think before speaking or acting.

What did you do today to observe this holiday?
Add any thoughts about your experience.

January 5
Get a Balanced Life Month-

The Bible passage I chose for today is
Ecclesiastes 3:1-8. Please, look it up and read it
aloud to the group.

Discuss how this Bible passage relates to today's
holiday.

Activity Suggestion:
1) Be kind to yourself and those around you by
taking care of yourself. Create a healthy balance in
your life between work and leisure.

What did you do today to observe this holiday?
Add any thoughts about your experience.

January 6
Adopt a Rescued Bird Month-

The Bible passage I chose for today is
Psalm 50:10-11. Please, look it up and read it aloud
to the group.

Discuss how this Bible passage relates to today's
holiday.

Activity Suggestions:
1) Set up a bird feeder outside to feed the birds
through the winter. One simple option is tying a
string to the top of a pine cone, covering it in
peanut butter, rolling it in seeds, and hanging it
from a tree.
2) Go for a nature walk (or spend some time
outside) and observe all the birds that you can.
Take the time to really look at and appreciate them.

What did you do today to observe this holiday?
Add any thoughts about your experience.

January 7
I'm Not Going to Take it Anymore Day-

The Bible passage I chose for today is
Romans 2:3-11. Please, look it up and read it aloud
to the group.

Discuss how this Bible passage relates to today's
holiday.

Activity Suggestion:
1) As Christians, we will put a new spin on this day.
Be patient and tolerant of others. Defend yourself
and set limits when needed, but with respect and
dignity to all involved.

What did you do today to observe this holiday?
Add any thoughts about your experience.

January 8
World Literacy Day-

The Bible passage I chose for today is
2 Timothy 3:16. Please, look it up and read it aloud
to the group.

Discuss how this Bible passage relates to today's
holiday.

Activity Suggestions:
1) Spend some time today reading the Bible.
2) If you do not have a Bible, is there someone you
can talk to about getting one, or at least having
access to one?
3) Spend some time reading something Christian or
other literature of decent values today.

What did you do today to observe this holiday?
Add any thoughts about your experience.

January 9
Law Enforcement Appreciation Day-

The Bible passage I chose for today is
Romans 13:1-4. Please, look it up and read it aloud
to the group.

Discuss how this Bible passage relates to today's
holiday.

Activity Suggestions:
1) Thank all law enforcement officers that you see
today for serving your community.
2) Send your local precinct a Thank You card.

What did you do today to observe this holiday?
Add any thoughts about your experience.

January 10
Universal Letter Writing Week-

The Bible passage I chose for today is
Proverbs 16:24. Please, look it up and read it aloud
to the group.

Discuss how this Bible passage relates to today's
holiday.

Activity Suggestion:
1) Write a kind letter, or send a card with a nice
handwritten message inside, to someone that you
believe is lonely or feels unappreciated.

What did you do today to observe this holiday?
Add any thoughts about your experience.

January 11
National Human Trafficking Awareness Day/
National Stalking Awareness Month/
National Codependency Awareness Month-

The Bible passage I chose for today is
Proverbs 31:8-9. Please, look it up and read it aloud
to the group.
*Note: If the version you read says "dumb", it does not mean
stupid. It means those who cannot talk.*

Discuss how this Bible passage relates to today's
holiday.

Activity Suggestions:
1) Combine these holidays by being aware of the
many ways people are abused, threatened, and
made to feel dependent upon others to further the
control and advantage.
2) Defend those in need.
3) Empower those you believe are victims by giving
them compliments and speaking kindly to them.
4) Offer help when appropriate, and connect them
with the proper resources for help.

What did you do today to observe this holiday?
Add any thoughts about your experience.

January 12
Be Kind to Food Servers Month-

The Bible passage I chose for today is
Romans 12:16. Please, look it up and read it aloud
to the group.

Discuss how this Bible passage relates to today's
holiday.

Activity Suggestion:
1) Give a special, genuine 'thank you' to all who
serve you, and always show respect to them.

What did you do today to observe this holiday?
Add any thoughts about your experience.

January 13
Blame Someone Else Day-

The Bible passage I chose for today is
Proverbs 28:13. Please, look it up and read it aloud
to the group.

Discuss how this Bible passage relates to today's
holiday.

Activity Suggestion:
1) Obviously, as Christians, we are going to turn
this one around. This will now be the day to make
an extra special point to take responsibility for what
we have done. If you still have something you have
not owned up to, this is as good a day as any.

What did you do today to observe this holiday?
Add any thoughts about your experience.

January 14
World Logic Day-

The Bible passage I chose for today is
1 Corinthians 14:20. Please, look it up and read it
aloud to the group.

Discuss how this Bible passage relates to today's
holiday.

Activity Suggestion:
1) Choose an issue you are experiencing, and
evaluate it in a logical manner. Write down your
thoughts about it. Determine goals and plans to
accomplish those goals.

What did you do today to observe this holiday?
Add any thoughts about your experience.

January 15
Celebration of Life Month-

The Bible passage I chose for today is
Proverbs 17:22. Please, look it up and read it aloud
to the group.

Discuss how this Bible passage relates to today's
holiday.

Activity Suggestions:
1) Be happy to be alive. Smell the roses. Appreciate
all the people and blessings in your life.
2) Smile at everyone you meet.

What did you do today to observe this holiday?
Add any thoughts about your experience.

January 16
National Day of Service-

The Bible passage I chose for today is Acts 20:35.
Please, look it up and read it aloud to the group.

Discuss how this Bible passage relates to today's
holiday.

Activity Suggestion:
1) Spend some time today serving others. Help
someone in some way.

What did you do today to observe this holiday?
Add any thoughts about your experience.

January 17
No Name Calling Week–

The Bible passage I chose for today is
Ephesians 4:29. Please, look it up and read it aloud
to the group.

Discuss how this Bible passage relates to today's
holiday.

Activity Suggestions:
1) Be very diligent this week in making sure that
you are not calling anyone names, or even implying
them. This means not even in joking. You never
know how jokes can actually hurt someone.
2) Do not laugh at the jokes of others that could
potentially hurt someone, and guide them, if you
can, into phrasing things a different way, or telling
different jokes.

What did you do today to observe this holiday?
Add any thoughts about your experience.

January 18
Week of Christian Unity-

The Bible passage I chose for today is John 13:35.
Please, look it up and read it aloud to the group.

Discuss how this Bible passage relates to today's
holiday.

Activity Suggestion:
1) Can people tell that you are a Christian without
you telling them, but by how you behave? If not,
what can you do to change that?

What did you do today to observe this holiday?
Add any thoughts about your experience.

January 19
Popcorn Day-

The Bible passage I chose for today is
1 Thessalonians 5:11. Please, look it up and read it
aloud to the group.

Discuss how this Bible passage relates to today's
holiday.

Activity Suggestion:
Make this a fun night with popcorn, friendship, and
a wholesome movie!

What did you do today to observe this holiday?
Add any thoughts about your experience.

January 20
Hunt for Happiness Week-

The Bible passage I chose for today is
Philippians 2:1-4. Please, look it up and read it
aloud to the group.

Discuss how this Bible passage relates to today's
holiday.

Activity Suggestion:
1) One of the best ways to be happy is to be a
blessing to someone else. Brighten someone else's
day, and you are likely to brighten your own.

What did you do today to observe this holiday?
Add any thoughts about your experience.

January 21
Squirrel Appreciation Day-

The Bible passage I chose for today is Genesis 1:26.
Please, look it up and read it aloud to the group.

Discuss how this Bible passage relates to today's
holiday.

Activity Suggestions:
1) Set up a squirrel feeder outside to feed the
squirrels through the winter. One simple option is
tying a string to the top of a pine cone, covering it
in peanut butter, rolling it in seeds, and hanging it
from a tree. Yes, just like for the birds. Just make
sure they can reach it from standing on a branch.
2) Go for a nature walk (or spend some time
outside) and observe all the squirrels that you can.
Take the time to really look at and appreciate them.

What did you do today to observe this holiday?
Add any thoughts about your experience.

January 22
Pro-Life Day-

The Bible passage I chose for today is
Psalm 139:13-14. Please, look it up and read it
aloud to the group.

Discuss how this Bible passage relates to today's
holiday.

Activity Suggestions:
1) Learn more about the stages of development of a
baby in the womb.
2) Advocate for the unborn when you can.

What did you do today to observe this holiday?
Add any thoughts about your experience.

January 23
National Handwriting Day-

The Bible passage I chose for today is
Galatians 6:11. Please, look it up and read it aloud
to the group.

Discuss how this Bible passage relates to today's
holiday.

Activity Suggestion:
1) Write a nice long letter to someone who would
appreciate hearing from you.

What did you do today to observe this holiday?
Add any thoughts about your experience.

January 24
National Compliment Day-

The Bible passage I chose for today is
Proverbs 12:25. Please, look it up and read it aloud
to the group.

Discuss how this Bible passage relates to today's
holiday.

Activity Suggestion:
1) Say something nice to as many people as you can
today. Make sure you are genuine. Never give out
fake compliments.

What did you do today to observe this holiday?
Add any thoughts about your experience.

January 25
National Clean Up Your Computer Month-

The Bible passage I chose for today is
Colossians 3:8. Please, look it up and read it aloud
to the group.

Discuss how this Bible passage relates to today's
holiday.

Activity Suggestion:
1) Go through your desktop, downloads, email, and
social media sites. Keep only clean and positive
stuff on your computer and social media, and delete
the rest.

What did you do today to observe this holiday?
Add any thoughts about your experience.

January 26
Shape Up US Month-

The Bible passage I chose for today is
1 Corinthians 6:19-20. Please, look it up and read it
aloud to the group.

Discuss how this Bible passage relates to today's
holiday.

Activity Suggestion:
1) Start being more health conscious for yourself
and your family. Make healthy food choices, and
take an opportunity to get in some exercise today.

What did you do today to observe this holiday?
Add any thoughts about your experience.

January 27
Holocaust Memorial Day (UK)-

The Bible passage I chose for today is 1 Peter 5:8. Please, look it up and read it aloud to the group.

Discuss how this Bible passage relates to today's holiday.

Activity Suggestion:
1) Learn about the Holocaust. Think about what lessons you can learn from that history. What can you do today to do your part in preventing something like that from happening again?

What did you do today to observe this holiday? Add any thoughts about your experience.

January 28
International Creativity Month-

The Bible passage I chose for today is
Romans 12:10-16. Please, look it up and read it
aloud to the group.

Discuss how this Bible passage relates to today's
holiday.

Activity Suggestion:
1) Think of a creative way to be a blessing to
others, and follow through.

What did you do today to observe this holiday?
Add any thoughts about your experience.

January 29
Curmudgeons Day-

The Bible passage I chose for today is
Proverbs 17:17. Please, look it up and read it aloud
to the group.

Discuss how this Bible passage relates to today's
holiday.

Activity Suggestion:
1) Find the most negative person you know, and
brighten his/her day.

What did you do today to observe this holiday?
Add any thoughts about your experience.

January 30
Bubble Wrap Appreciation Day-

The Bible passage I chose for today is
Ecclesiastes 3:1-8. Please, look it up and read it
aloud to the group.
*Note: This one may take a little planning to get ahold of
enough bubble wrap for everyone to dance on. It comes in
many packages, so it can be saved and used for this. You
could ask your coworkers to start saving it today and use it
when you have enough.*

Discuss how this Bible passage relates to today's
holiday.

Activity Suggestion:
1) Buy some bubble wrap (or pull some out that
you have saved from a package), lay it on a hard
floor, turn on some music and have a dance party
on bubble wrap.

What did you do today to observe this holiday?
Add any thoughts about your experience.

January 31
National Mentoring Month-

The Bible passage I chose for today is 1 Peter 5:1-5. Please, look it up and read it aloud to the group.

Discuss how this Bible passage relates to today's holiday.

Activity Suggestion:
1) Be a mentor for someone, officially or unofficially. Guide those who could benefit from your time and experience.

What did you do today to observe this holiday? Add any thoughts about your experience.

3
FEBRUARY

February 1
National Get Up Day-

The Bible passage I chose for today is
Romans 12:11. Please, look it up and read it aloud
to the group.

Discuss how this Bible passage relates to today's
holiday.

Activity Suggestions:
1) Get some exercise today.
2) Do something today that you have been putting
off.
3) Do what you can to spend the day active and
motivated.

What did you do today to observe this holiday?
Add any thoughts about your experience.

February 2
Self-Renewal Day-

The Bible passage I chose for today is
Colossians 3:8-10. Please, look it up and read it
aloud to the group.

Discuss how this Bible passage relates to today's
holiday.

Activity Suggestion:
1) This is a good time to think about the changes
you would like to make within yourself and your
life. Write it down so you can be detailed and
specific, and so that you can refer to it as a
reminder.

What did you do today to observe this holiday?
Add any thoughts about your experience.

February 3
National Hot Breakfast Month-

The Bible passage I chose for today is 3 John 1:2. Please, look it up and read it aloud to the group.

Discuss how this Bible passage relates to today's holiday.

Activity Suggestion:
1) If you have a choice between a hot and cold breakfast this morning, choose the hot one, and encourage your friends to do the same.

What did you do today to observe this holiday? Add any thoughts about your experience.

February 4
National Thank a Mail Carrier Day-

The Bible passage I chose for today is
1 Thessalonians 1:2. Please, look it up and read it
aloud to the group.

Discuss how this Bible passage relates to today's
holiday.

Activity Suggestions:
1) Thank your mail carrier if you see him/her.
2) Make a thank you card for your mail carrier and
set it out in the mail. Make sure it's on top and
clearly labeled.

What did you do today to observe this holiday?
Add any thoughts about your experience.

February 5
National Mend a Broken Heart Month-

The Bible passage I chose for today is John 16:22.
Please, look it up and read it aloud to the group.

Discuss how this Bible passage relates to today's
holiday.

Activity Suggestions:
1) Make some time to spend with someone who
has been recently hurt.
2) If you have been recently hurt, find someone
trusted to talk to.

What did you do today to observe this holiday?
Add any thoughts about your experience.

February 6
Pay a Compliment Day-

The Bible passage I chose for today is
Proverbs 12:25. Please, look it up and read it aloud
to the group.

Discuss how this Bible passage relates to today's
holiday.

Activity Suggestion:
1) Give a genuine compliment to someone, ideally
someone you may generally overlook.

What did you do today to observe this holiday?
Add any thoughts about your experience.

February 7
National Therapeutic Recreation Month-

The Bible passage I chose for today is
Galatians 5:14. Please, look it up and read it aloud
to the group.

Discuss how this Bible passage relates to today's
holiday.

Activity Suggestion:
1) Participate in a fun activity with someone who is
struggling/recovering mentally, physically, or
emotionally.

What did you do today to observe this holiday?
Add any thoughts about your experience.

February 8
Burn Awareness Week (1st full week)-

The Bible passage I chose for today is
Proverbs 27:12. Please, look it up and read it aloud
to the group.

Discuss how this Bible passage relates to today's
holiday.

Activity Suggestion:
1) Make yourself and others aware of burn safety
prevention tips, first aid for burns, and when to
seek medical help.

What did you do today to observe this holiday?
Add any thoughts about your experience.

February 9
National Stop Bullying Day-

The Bible passage I chose for today is
Proverbs 6:16-19. Please, look it up and read it
aloud to the group.

Discuss how this Bible passage relates to today's
holiday.

Activity Suggestion:
1) As a group, watch a movie that advocates against
bullying. (I believe *The Secrets of Jonathan Sperry* is a
good movie for this).

What did you do today to observe this holiday?
Add any thoughts about your experience.

February 10
All the News That's Fit to Print Day-

The Bible passage I chose for today is Exodus 23:1.
Please, look it up and read it aloud to the group.

Discuss how this Bible passage relates to today's
holiday.

Activity Suggestions:
1) Absolutely REFUSE to listen to any gossip, and
certainly do not spread any.
2) Verify anything that you read that makes claims
that may mislead people. Avoid sources that
mislead people or disparage others.

What did you do today to observe this holiday?
Add any thoughts about your experience.

February 11
Make a Friend's Day -

The Bible passage I chose for today is 1 Peter 5:5.
Please, look it up and read it aloud to the group.

Discuss how this Bible passage relates to today's
holiday.

Activity Suggestion:
1) Do something to be a blessing to someone else
today.

What did you do today to observe this holiday?
Add any thoughts about your experience.

February 12
No One Eats Alone Day-

The Bible passage I chose for today is
Ecclesiastes 4:9-12. Please, look it up and read it
aloud to the group.

Discuss how this Bible passage relates to today's
holiday.

Activity Suggestion:
1) Ask to sit with anyone who is eating alone, or
invite them to sit with you.

What did you do today to observe this holiday?
Add any thoughts about your experience.

February 13
Desperation Day-

The Bible passage I chose for today is
Proverbs 17:17. Please, look it up and read it aloud
to the group.

Discuss how this Bible passage relates to today's
holiday.

Activity Suggestion:
1) Give companionship to someone who feels
alone.

What did you do today to observe this holiday?
Add any thoughts about your experience.

February 14
Safer Internet Day (2nd Th.)-

The Bible passage I chose for today is
Galatians 5:19-21. Please, look it up and read it
aloud to the group.
*Note: It says those who DO, not those who DID these
things. We always have the chance to repent, which is to turn
away from those things and make better choices.*

Discuss how this Bible passage relates to today's
holiday.

Activity Suggestions:
1) Help monitor to make sure your children are not
exposed to inappropriate sites. Use parental blocks
when appropriate.
2) Do not use any inappropriate sites yourself.
Show that those blocks protect ALL of us from
inappropriate material.

What did you do today to observe this holiday?
Add any thoughts about your experience.

February 15
Random Acts of Kindness Day (Wed. of 2ⁿᵈ full week)/Children of Alcoholics Week (2ⁿᵈ full week)-

The Bible passage I chose for today is Proverbs 23:29-35. Please, look it up and read it aloud to the group.

Discuss how this Bible passage relates to today's holiday.

Activity Suggestions:
1) Perform a random act of kindness to a child/children of parents struggling with addiction. If you do not know anyone in this situation, perform a random act of kindness to anyone.
2) If you are that parent, do something special for your children today.

What did you do today to observe this holiday? Add any thoughts about your experience.

February 16
National Parent Leadership Month-

The Bible passage I chose for today is
Proverbs 22:6. Please, look it up and read it aloud
to the group.

Discuss how this Bible passage relates to today's
holiday.

Activity Suggestions:
1) If you are a parent, be conscious of the example
you are setting.
2) Take your next opportunity to casually strike up
a conversation with your child(ren) about their lives
and what is important to them.
3) If you are not a parent, is there a child you know
that could benefit from some time, a listening ear,
and some good advice?

What did you do today to observe this holiday?
Add any thoughts about your experience.

February 17
My Way Day/International Friendship Week-

The Bible passage I chose for today is
Proverbs 11:24-25. Please, look it up and read it
aloud to the group.

Discuss how this Bible passage relates to today's
holiday.

Activity Suggestion:
1) As Christians, we will put a spin on My Way Day
and focus more on friendship. Let your friend pick
the movie, music, or activity today (as long as it is
moral and legal), and do so with a happy heart.

What did you do today to observe this holiday?
Add any thoughts about your experience.

February 18
Thumb Appreciation Day-

The Bible passage I chose for today is
Psalm 139:14. Please, look it up and read it aloud to
the group.

Discuss how this Bible passage relates to today's
holiday.

Activity Suggestion:
1) Spend the day doing your best to avoid using
your thumbs (when you can do so safely and not
when you are expected to work, do homework, or
things like that where people are counting on you
to do your best). We take many things for granted
and it is good to realize those things sometimes.

What did you do today to observe this holiday?
Add any thoughts about your experience.

February 19
 Day-

The Bible passage I chose for today is
Proverbs 18:24. Please, look it up and read it aloud
to the group.

Discuss how this Bible passage relates to today's
holiday.

Activity Suggestions:
1) Call or write your best friend today. Let them
know how much you appreciate them.
2) This is also a good day to evaluate who your real
friends are, and if you are a real friend to others.
(We do not want to give up on people, but we need
to be able to make decisions about boundaries to
set for unhealthy friends. It is also possible that
some unhealthy friends just may have never
experienced, or been taught, any better. So, some
love, patience, boundaries, and modeling could go a
long way.)

What did you do today to observe this holiday?
Add any thoughts about your experience.

February 20
Through with the Chew (3rd full week)-

The Bible passage I chose for today is
1 Corinthians 6:19-20. Please, look it up and read it
aloud to the group.

Discuss how this Bible passage relates to today's
holiday.

Activity Suggestions:
1) If you chew tobacco, make a plan to quit,
including gathering up a support system.
2) If you know someone who chews tobacco, offer
to be that support.

What did you do today to observe this holiday?
Add any thoughts about your experience.

February 21
National Time Management Month/Plant the
Seeds of Greatness Month-

The Bible passage I chose for today is
Matthew 22:34-40. Please, look it up and read it
aloud to the group.

Discuss how this Bible passage relates to today's
holiday.

Activity Suggestion:
1) Plan what is the best use of your time to
accomplish your goals, especially those of your
relationships with God and other people.

What did you do today to observe this holiday?
Add any thoughts about your experience.

February 22
Inconvenience Yourself Day (4ᵗʰ Wed.)-

The Bible passage I chose for today is
Philippians 2:1-4. Please, look it up and read it
aloud to the group.

Discuss how this Bible passage relates to today's
holiday.

Activity Suggestion:
1) Go out of your way to help someone today, and
do it with a joyful heart.

What did you do today to observe this holiday?
Add any thoughts about your experience.

February 23
National Eating Disorders Awareness Week-

The Bible passage I chose for today is James 3:6.
Please, look it up and read it aloud to the group.

Discuss how this Bible passage relates to today's
holiday.

Activity Suggestions:
1) Do not judge or discuss someone's body size and
shape (unless they are specifically asking you for
advice, and then, still be kind).
2) Do not make jokes about body shapes and sizes,
and don't laugh at the jokes of others that do so.

What did you do today to observe this holiday?
Add any thoughts about your experience.

February 24
National Dance Day-

The Bible passage I chose for today is
Psalm 30:11-12. Please, look it up and read it aloud
to the group.

Discuss how this Bible passage relates to today's
holiday.

Activity Suggestion:
1) Play some appropriate music and dance.

What did you do today to observe this holiday?
Add any thoughts about your experience.

February 25
Relationship Wellness Month-

The Bible passage I chose for today is
Ephesians 5:25-29. Please, look it up and read it
aloud to the group.

Discuss how this Bible passage relates to today's
holiday.

Activity Suggestions:
1) Only stay in a healthy relationship.
2) If you are married, get the appropriate help for
any unhealthy behaviors.
3) If you know someone in an unhealthy
relationship, be the supportive friend that they
need.

What did you do today to observe this holiday?
Add any thoughts about your experience.

February 26
World Pistachio Day-

The Bible passage I chose for today is
Ecclesiastes 2:24-25. Please, look it up and read it
aloud to the group.

Discuss how this Bible passage relates to today's
holiday.

Activity Suggestion:
1) Enjoy pistachio pudding or another pistachio
treat together as a group. Eating together often
promotes good conversation.

What did you do today to observe this holiday?
Add any thoughts about your experience.

February 27
National Retro Day-

The Bible passage I chose for today is
Ecclesiastes 3:12-13. Please, look it up and read it
aloud to the group.

Discuss how this Bible passage relates to today's
holiday.

Activity Suggestion:
1) Spend some time today sharing positive
memories from days gone by.

What did you do today to observe this holiday?
Add any thoughts about your experience.

February 28
National Science Day-

The Bible passage I chose for today is
Psalm 111:2. Please, look it up and read it aloud to
the group.

Discuss how this Bible passage relates to today's
holiday.

Activity Suggestions:
1) Do a science experiment as a group.
2) Learn some fun scientific facts.
3) Watch a science show together.
Note: Make sure the science you explore is not based upon
theories that go against Bible teachings, and cannot be
proven, such as evolution and an old Earth.

What did you do today to observe this holiday?
Add any thoughts about your experience.

February 29
World Rare Disease Day-

The Bible passage I chose for today is
Matthew 8:2-4. Please, look it up and read it aloud
to the group.

Discuss how this Bible passage relates to today's
holiday.

Activity Suggestion:
1) Learn about a rare illness, and then spread
awareness about it on social media or in person.

What did you do today to observe this holiday?
Add any thoughts about your experience.

4

MARCH

March 1
World Compliment Day/Zero Discrimination Day-

The Bible passage I chose for today is
Proverbs 12:25. Please, look it up and read it aloud
to the group.

Discuss how this Bible passage relates to today's
holiday.

Activity Suggestion:
1) Give a genuine compliment to someone, ideally
someone you may generally overlook.

What did you do today to observe this holiday?
Add any thoughts about your experience.

March 2
National Write a Letter of Appreciation Week-

The Bible passage I chose for today is
Philippians 1:3. Please, look it up and read it aloud
to the group.

Discuss how this Bible passage relates to today's
holiday.

Activity Suggestion:
1) Choose someone you appreciate, that may not
feel appreciated, and get to writing!

What did you do today to observe this holiday?
Add any thoughts about your experience.

March 3
I Want You to Be Happy Day-

The Bible passage I chose for today is
Matthew 5:16. Please, look it up and read it aloud to
the group.

Discuss how this Bible passage relates to today's
holiday.

Activity Suggestion:
1) Try to make a wish of someone else come true,
no matter how small.

What did you do today to observe this holiday?
Add any thoughts about your experience.

March 4
Courageous Follower Day/March Forth and
Do Something Day-

The Bible passage I chose for today is
1 Samuel 25:25-26. Please, look it up and read it
aloud to the group.
Note: You may want to read the entire chapter 25 for the
full story of what was going on between David, Nabal, and
Abigail.

Discuss how this Bible passage relates to today's
holiday.

Activity Suggestion:
1) This is the day to stand up to and for our leaders.
Make sure you do so in a very respectful manner.

What did you do today to observe this holiday?
Add any thoughts about your experience.

March 5
National Procrastination Week-

The Bible passage I chose for today is
Proverbs 6:6-8. Please, look it up and read it aloud
to the group.

Discuss how this Bible passage relates to today's
holiday.

Activity Suggestion:
1) What have you been putting off? Take steps to
do it today.

What did you do today to observe this holiday?
Add any thoughts about your experience.

March 6
National March into Literacy Month-

The Bible passage I chose for today is
2 Timothy 3:16-17. Please, look it up and read it
aloud to the group.

Discuss how this Bible passage relates to today's
holiday.

Activity Suggestion:
1) Go to the library and select a book you would
like to read. It would be wonderful if you would
select a Christian book to read.

What did you do today to observe this holiday?
Add any thoughts about your experience.

March 7
World Math Day-

The Bible passage I chose for today is
Proverbs 18:15. Please, look it up and read it aloud
to the group.

Discuss how this Bible passage relates to today's
holiday.

Activity Suggestions:
1) Play a math game online, such as Sudoku.
2) Play a game that involves numbers with the
group. It could be a board game, card game, one
found in a book, online, etc.
3) Have a group on finances, such as skills in
balancing a checkbook.

What did you do today to observe this holiday?
Add any thoughts about your experience.

March 8
Day for Women's Rights & International Peace-

The Bible passage I chose for today is
Luke 13:10-17. Please, look it up and read it aloud
to the group.

Discuss how this Bible passage relates to today's
holiday.

Activity Suggestion:
1) Spend some time today learning about women's
rights issues, including in other countries, and
choose some way to help.

What did you do today to observe this holiday?
Add any thoughts about your experience.

March 9
Get over It Day/Panic Day/National Words Matter Week-

The Bible passage I chose for today is
2 Corinthians 4:7-9. Please, look it up and read it
aloud to the group.

Discuss how this Bible passage relates to today's
holiday.

Activity Suggestions:
1) Determine what you've been stressing over that
you need to let go, and then let it go.
2) Be extra careful of the words you use when you
feel stressed.

What did you do today to observe this holiday?
Add any thoughts about your experience.

March 10
International Day of Awesomeness-

The Bible passage I chose for today is
Proverbs 19:17. Please, look it up and read it aloud
to the group.

Discuss how this Bible passage relates to today's
holiday.

Activity Suggestion:
1) Do something today to help someone less
fortunate than you are.

What did you do today to observe this holiday?
Add any thoughts about your experience.

March 11
Dream Day-

The Bible passage I chose for today is James 2:16.
Please, look it up and read it aloud to the group.

Discuss how this Bible passage relates to today's
holiday.

Activity Suggestion:
1) Determine today to make one dream of someone
else come true (no matter how small).

What did you do today to observe this holiday?
Add any thoughts about your experience.

March 12
National Nutrition Month/National Athletic Training Month-

The Bible passage I chose for today is
1 Corinthians 6:19-20. Please, look it up and read it
aloud to the group.

Discuss how this Bible passage relates to today's
holiday.

Activity Suggestion:
1) Make a healthy picnic lunch, head to the park (or
other outdoor area), and play an outdoor game with
your group.

What did you do today to observe this holiday?
Add any thoughts about your experience.

March 13
Good Samaritan Involvement Day

The Bible passage I chose for today is
Luke 10:25-37. Please, look it up and read it aloud
to the group.

Discuss how this Bible passage relates to today's
holiday.

Activity Suggestion:
1) Find a way to be of help to someone today.

What did you do today to observe this holiday?
Add any thoughts about your experience.

March 14
Write Your Story Day-

The Bible passage I chose for today is 2 Peter 3:1.
Please, look it up and read it aloud to the group.

Discuss how this Bible passage relates to today's
holiday.

Activity Suggestion:
1) Choose an episode from your life that could be
an inspiration to others, and write it down.

What did you do today to observe this holiday?
Add any thoughts about your experience.

March 15
National Everything You Think Is Wrong Day-

The Bible passage I chose for today is
Proverbs 18:17. Please, look it up and read it aloud
to the group.

Discuss how this Bible passage relates to today's
holiday.

Activity Suggestion:
1) Think about a situation in your life, or that which
you comment on social media, of which you are
sure you know who is right. Now, spend some time
thinking about, and writing down, all the ways your
thinking could be wrong. What could you not know
about the situation? In what circumstances could
the other person be right? What may have
happened in the past that would make that person's
position more understandable? Keep asking and
answering questions like this. These things you are
supposing now may not be true at all, but it helps
to realize that there are many things we do not
know that could change our perception of the
situation, or at least make us more kind in our
reactions.

What did you do today to observe this holiday?
Add any thoughts about your experience.

March 16
Youth Art Month/National Craft Month-
Engage children close to you in an art/craft project today.

The Bible passage I chose for today is Exodus 35:30-35. Please, look it up and read it aloud to the group.

Discuss how this Bible passage relates to today's holiday.

Activity Suggestions:
1) Engage children close to you in an art/craft project today.
2) Choose any artistic and/or craft project you can work on yourself or with others. This may be something you already enjoy, or something you have never tried before. You may choose to keep your creation or bless someone else with it.

What did you do today to observe this holiday? Add any thoughts about your experience.

March 17
National Ethics Awareness Month-

The Bible passage I chose for today is
Exodus 20:1-17. Please, look it up and read it aloud
to the group.

Discuss how this Bible passage relates to today's
holiday.

Activity Suggestion:
1) Be aware of the ethical issues around you: in
person, on the news, and the television shows you
watch. When you make yourself aware of what is
going on, you have a much better chance of staying
on the right side of things, and maybe even help to
change things for the better.

What did you do today to observe this holiday?
Add any thoughts about your experience.

March 18
Awkward Moments Day/Forgive Mom and Dad Day-

The Bible passage I chose for today is
Ephesians 4:31. Please, look it up and read it aloud
to the group.

Discuss how this Bible passage relates to today's
holiday.

Activity Suggestion:
1) It's time to end the awkwardness. Forgive who
you need to forgive, and move on for a better today
and future.

What did you do today to observe this holiday?
Add any thoughts about your experience.

March 19
**National Animal Poison Prevention Week (3ʳᵈ
full week)/National Inhalant and Poisons
Awareness Week-**

The Bible passage I chose for today is Genesis 1:26.
Please, look it up and read it aloud to the group.

Discuss how this Bible passage relates to today's
holiday.

Activity Suggestion:
1) Become aware of the poisons to people, animals,
plants, and soil. Guard against each when you can.

What did you do today to observe this holiday?
Add any thoughts about your experience.

March 20
Well-Elderly Day (3ʳᵈ Wed.)/World Storytelling Day (Spring Equinox)/Won't You Be My Neighbor Day-

The Bible passage I chose for today is Leviticus 19:32. Please, look it up and read it aloud to the group.

Discuss how this Bible passage relates to today's holiday.

Activity Suggestions:
1) Engage an elderly relative or neighbor in a conversation about their younger days. They have many interesting stories to tell.
2) Write a letter or call an elderly relative or other elderly person that you know.
3) If you are an elderly person, spend some time talking with a younger relative or neighbor.
4) If you are an elderly person, share stories with another elderly friend, neighbor, or relative.

What did you do today to observe this holiday? Add any thoughts about your experience.

March 21
National Common Courtesy Day-

The Bible passage I chose for today is
1 Corinthians 13:3-7. Please, look it up and read it
aloud to the group.

Discuss how this Bible passage relates to today's
holiday.

Activity Suggestions:
1) Make a special effort to be courteous to everyone
today.
2) Discuss ways in which people may be
thoughtless and rude unintentionally, and how to
be more mindful to treat others courteously.

What did you do today to observe this holiday?
Add any thoughts about your experience.

March 22
National Sing Out Day-

The Bible passage I chose for today is James 5:13.
Please, look it up and read it aloud to the group.

Discuss how this Bible passage relates to today's
holiday.

Activity Suggestions:
1) Choose some songs (appropriate ones) and sing
as a group.
2) Listen to music and sing along.

What did you do today to observe this holiday?
Add any thoughts about your experience.

March 23
National Agriculture Day-

The Bible passage I chose for today is Genesis 1:29. Please, look it up and read it aloud to the group.

Discuss how this Bible passage relates to today's holiday.

Activity Suggestions:
1) If you have an opportunity, thank a farmer.
2) Learn something about the issues facing farmers today.
3) Learn something about gardening/farming.

What did you do today to observe this holiday? Add any thoughts about your experience.

March 24
Education and Sharing Day-

The Bible passage I chose for today is Proverbs 9:9.
Please, look it up and read it aloud to the group.

Discuss how this Bible passage relates to today's
holiday.

Activity Suggestions:
1) Take the time to share your knowledge with
someone who wants to learn something you can
teach.
2) Let someone teach you something.

What did you do today to observe this holiday?
Add any thoughts about your experience.

March 25
International Day of Remembrance of the
Victims of Slavery -

The Bible passage I chose for today is
Exodus 21:16. Please, look it up and read it aloud
to the group.

Discuss how this Bible passage relates to today's
holiday.

Activity Suggestions:
1) Educate yourself on current issues of slavery,
and how you can help to end that today.
2) Do not look at or watch any pornography. Get
rid of any pornographic magazines that you may
have, and delete all inappropriate materials from
your computer and phone.
3) Do not listen to any music or watch any shows
that are demeaning to anyone.

What did you do today to observe this holiday?
Add any thoughts about your experience.

March 26
Week of Solidarity with People Struggling Against Racism & Discrimination-

The Bible passage I chose for today is Isaiah 1:17. Please, look it up and read it aloud to the group.

Discuss how this Bible passage relates to today's holiday.

Activity Suggestion:
1) Stand up for those you see being treated unfairly. (Make sure your actions are legal and moral.)

What did you do today to observe this holiday? Add any thoughts about your experience.

March 27
Act Happy Week (starts on 3rd Wed.)/
Optimism Month/Spiritual Wellness Month-

The Bible passage I chose for today is
Psalm 34:1-3. Please, look it up and read it aloud to
the group.

Discuss how this Bible passage relates to today's
holiday.

Activity Suggestion:
1) Spend the entire day seeing the positive in
everything you can.

What did you do today to observe this holiday?
Add any thoughts about your experience.

March 28
Virtual Advocacy Day-

The Bible passage I chose for today is
Proverbs 15:1-4. Please, look it up and read it aloud
to the group.

Discuss how this Bible passage relates to today's
holiday.

Activity Suggestion:
1) On social media sites, stand up for those being
belittled, and do it in a way that won't offend, but
will change the perspective and tone of what is
being said and done.

What did you do today to observe this holiday?
Add any thoughts about your experience.

March 29
Smoke and Mirrors Day-

The Bible passage I chose for today is
Matthew 24:23-24. Please, look it up and read it
aloud to the group.

Discuss how this Bible passage relates to today's
holiday.

Activity Suggestions:
1) Discuss ways in which people are deceived.
2) Verify the truth in what you see and hear. Seek
out the original sources. If it is something online,
try to verify it with 3 separate sources.

What did you do today to observe this holiday?
Add any thoughts about your experience.

March 30
**Grass is Always Browner on the Other Side of
the Fence Day/I Am in Control Day-**

The Bible passage I chose for today is
Proverbs 14:1. Please, look it up and read it aloud
to the group.

Discuss how this Bible passage relates to today's
holiday.

Activity Suggestion:
1) Realize that it is the grass you water that grows.
Spend some time today watering that grass.

What did you do today to observe this holiday?
Add any thoughts about your experience.

March 31
National Crayon Day-

The Bible passage I chose for today is
Matthew 11:28-29. Please, look it up and read it
aloud to the group.

Discuss how this Bible passage relates to today's
holiday.

Activity Suggestion:
1) Spend some time coloring today. It can be very
relaxing.

What did you do today to observe this holiday?
Add any thoughts about your experience.

5

APRIL

April 1
National Fun Day/Golden Rule Week-

The Bible passage I chose for today is
Matthew 7:12. Please, look it up and read it aloud to
the group.

Discuss how this Bible passage relates to today's
holiday.

Activity Suggestion:
1) Plan a fun activity with your group today. Play
fairly and treat everyone with respect.

What did you do today to observe this holiday?
Add any thoughts about your experience.

April 2
Reconciliation Day-

The Bible passages I chose for today are
Matthew 5:23-24 and Matthew 18:15-17. Please,
look them up and read them aloud to the group.

Discuss how this Bible passage relates to today's
holiday.

Activity Suggestion:
1) Think of someone with whom you haven't been
getting along well and contact them to make peace.

What did you do today to observe this holiday?
Add any thoughts about your experience.

April 3
Weed Out Hate: Sow the Seeds of Greatness
Day-

The Bible passage I chose for today is
Matthew 5:43-48. Please, look it up and read it
aloud to the group.

Discuss how this Bible passage relates to today's
holiday.

Activity Suggestions:
1) When you notice yourself having hateful feelings,
stop and pray for a better perspective. Do a
kindness for that person instead.
2) Find something to bring you joy and give you a
laugh (NOT laughing AT anyone).

What did you do today to observe this holiday?
Add any thoughts about your experience.

April 4
Victims of Violence Day/Hate Week-

The Bible passage I chose for today is Psalm 11:5. Please, look it up and read it aloud to the group.

Discuss how this Bible passage relates to today's holiday.

Activity Suggestion:
1) Think about how you handle anger. Are there any ways that you could improve? What steps can you take today? Do you need help? Do not be afraid to admit it and get the help you need.

What did you do today to observe this holiday? Add any thoughts about your experience.

April 5
National Dandelion Day-

The Bible passage I chose for today is
Song of Solomon 2:12. Please, look it up and read it
aloud to the group.

Discuss how this Bible passage relates to today's
holiday.

Activity Suggestions:
1) Learn about dandelions, especially the health
benefits.
2) Go for a walk and enjoy the beauty of this
wonderful flower.

What did you do today to observe this holiday?
Add any thoughts about your experience.

April 6
Jump over Things Day-

The Bible passage I chose for today is
Philippians 4:13. Please, look it up and read it aloud
to the group.

Discuss how this Bible passage relates to today's
holiday.

Activity Suggestions:
1) Set up a mini obstacle course with a few things
to go around, over, and under. How can you use
these types of skills for obstacles in your life?
2) Set up increasingly taller objects to jump over.
See how high you can jump.

What did you do today to observe this holiday?
Add any thoughts about your experience.

April 7
Emotional Overeating Awareness Month-

The Bible passage I chose for today is 3 John 1:2.
Please, look it up and read it aloud to the group.

Discuss how this Bible passage relates to today's
holiday.

Activity Suggestion:
1) When you are feeling emotional, think about
what you are eating and drinking. What can you do
to make yourself feel better that is actually good for
you? Do that.

What did you do today to observe this holiday?
Add any thoughts about your experience.

April 8
National Dog Fighting Awareness Day-

The Bible passage I chose for today is
Proverbs 12:10. Please, look it up and read it aloud
to the group.

Discuss how this Bible passage relates to today's
holiday.

Activity Suggestion:
1) Do NOT support dog fighting in any way.
Educate yourself on the issue.

What did you do today to observe this holiday?
Add any thoughts about your experience.

April 9
National Chicken Little Awareness Day-

The Bible passage I chose for today is
Zephaniah 3:17. Please, look it up and read it aloud
to the group.

Discuss how this Bible passage relates to today's
holiday.

Activity Suggestion:
1) Read the story of Chicken Little. Do you see
yourself in any of the characters? What are the
lessons that can be learned from the story?

What did you do today to observe this holiday?
Add any thoughts about your experience.

April 10
National Catch and Release Day-

The Bible passage I chose for today is
Philippians 4:8. Please, look it up and read it aloud
to the group.

Discuss how this Bible passage relates to today's
holiday.

Activity Suggestions:
1) Write out this verse so that you can use it as a
reminder.
2) Use paint, colors, markers, etc. to write out the
thinking list words in an artistic manner to display
and remind yourself what to think about.
3) Play catch and release with your thoughts. If you
get a thought that is not on the list, treat it like the
fish too small to keep. Throw it back and try for
another thought, something worth thinking about.

What did you do today to observe this holiday?
Add any thoughts about your experience.

April 11
Global Day to End Child Sexual Abuse (2ⁿᵈ Th.)-

The Bible passage I chose for today is
Psalm 82:3-4. Please, look it up and read it aloud to
the group.

Discuss how this Bible passage relates to today's
holiday.

Activity Suggestions:
1) Educate yourself on the issue.
2) If you know about it happening, report it.
3) Provide any help you can to victims, and also to
perpetrators to get them the professional help they
need to change.
4) If you are a victim or perpetrator, seek help.

What did you do today to observe this holiday?
Add any thoughts about your experience.

April 12
National Sexually Transmitted Diseases
Education and Awareness Month-

The Bible passage I chose for today is
1 Corinthians 3:16-17. Please, look it up and read it
aloud to the group.

Discuss how this Bible passage relates to today's
holiday.

Activity Suggestion:
1) Spend some time learning about STD's and how
to prevent them. Also learn how to detect and treat
them, and seek medical attention if there is any
indication you may need it.

What did you do today to observe this holiday?
Add any thoughts about your experience.

April 13
Undiagnosed Children's Awareness Day-

The Bible passage I chose for today is
Proverbs 2:1-5. Please, look it up and read it aloud
to the group.

Discuss how this Bible passage relates to today's
holiday.

Activity Suggestions:
1) Be kind to everyone, as we do not always know
their situations.
2) Learn the signs to look for when children may
need to see a doctor.
3) Pray for doctors to have the wisdom needed to
diagnose and treat the children, and for the
caregivers to know when to take their children to
the doctor or specialist.

What did you do today to observe this holiday?
Add any thoughts about your experience.

April 14
National Humor Month-

The Bible passage I chose for today is
Proverbs 17:22. Please, look it up and read it aloud
to the group.

Discuss how this Bible passage relates to today's
holiday.

Activity Suggestion:
1) Enjoy some jokes and/or a funny movie. Make
sure the jokes are not offensive to anyone, and the
movie is wholesome.

What did you do today to observe this holiday?
Add any thoughts about your experience.

April 15
Stress Awareness Month-

The Bible passage I chose for today is John 14:27.
Please, look it up and read it aloud to the group.

Discuss how this Bible passage relates to today's
holiday.

Activity Suggestions:
1) Do something today to remove some stress from
someone's life.
2) Do something today to remove some stress from
your life.
3) Learn some healthy ways to deal with stress.

What did you do today to observe this holiday?
Add any thoughts about your experience.

April 16
Jazz Appreciation Month-

The Bible passage I chose for today is Psalm 95:1.
Please, look it up and read it aloud to the group.

Discuss how this Bible passage relates to today's
holiday.

Activity Suggestion:
1) Listen to jazz music with your group. There is
Christian jazz music, too.

What did you do today to observe this holiday?
Add any thoughts about your experience.

April 17
World Circus Day-

The Bible passage I chose for today is
Proverbs 17:22. Please, look it up and read it aloud
to the group.

Discuss how this Bible passage relates to today's
holiday.

Activity Suggestions:
1) Watch a circus performance online or on
television.
2) Everyone in the group, choose a circus-like
activity to practice and perform. Ideas could include
juggling, walking on a thin beam, pretending to be a
mime, etc. Use your imagination and have fun.

What did you do today to observe this holiday?
Add any thoughts about your experience.

April 18
National Newspaper Columnists Day-

The Bible passages I chose for today are
Proverbs 25:25 and Psalm 112:7. Please, look them
up and read them aloud to the group.

Discuss how these Bible passages relate to today's
holiday.

Activity Suggestion:
1) Have each member of the group read an article
from the newspaper and share what they learned.

What did you do today to observe this holiday?
Add any thoughts about your experience.

April 19
Listening Awareness Month-

The Bible passage I chose for today is
James 1:19. Please, look it up and read it aloud to
the group.

Discuss how this Bible passage relates to today's
holiday.

Activity Suggestion:
1) Make a conscious effort all day to let someone
completely finish speaking, and then think carefully
about what they said before answering. Do not
interrupt anyone, and do not spend the time they
are speaking thinking about your rebuttal.

What did you do today to observe this holiday?
Add any thoughts about your experience.

April 20
**Police Officers Who Gave Their Lives in the
Line of Duty Week-**

The Bible passage I chose for today is John 15:13.
Please, look it up and read it aloud to the group.

Discuss how this Bible passage relates to today's
holiday.

Activity Suggestions:
1) If you know of a fallen officer, find a way to
honor him/her.
2) Post a tribute to law enforcement on social
media.

What did you do today to observe this holiday?
Add any thoughts about your experience.

April 21
Big Word Day-

The Bible passage I chose for today is
Proverbs 18:15. Please, look it up and read it aloud
to the group.

Discuss how this Bible passage relates to today's
holiday.

Activity Suggestion:
1) Look up and learn a new vocabulary word. Try
to find a way to use it today. If everyone shares
their words with the group, you will all learn many
new words.

What did you do today to observe this holiday?
Add any thoughts about your experience.

April 22
Earth Day-

The Bible passage I chose for today is
Psalm 24:1-2. Please, look it up and read it aloud to
the group.

Discuss how this Bible passage relates to today's
holiday.

Activity Suggestions:
1) Think of what you can do to make the Earth a
better place.
2) Picking up trash around your neighborhood or
local park may be a good place to start. As always,
take necessary precautions.

What did you do today to observe this holiday?
Add any thoughts about your experience.

April 23
World Book Night-

The Bible passage I chose for today is
Philippians 4:8. Please, look it up and read it aloud
to the group.

Discuss how this Bible passage relates to today's
holiday.

Activity Suggestion:
1) Choose a good book to read tonight. Be sure
that it meets the criteria in the passage.

What did you do today to observe this holiday?
Add any thoughts about your experience.

April 24
National Volunteer Week-

The Bible passage I chose for today is
Hebrews 6:10-12. Please, look it up and read it
aloud to the group.

Discuss how this Bible passage relates to today's
holiday.

Activity Suggestion:
1) Volunteer your time to help out where you are,
or to help someone who is also there.

What did you do today to observe this holiday?
Add any thoughts about your experience.

April 25
Community Spirit Day/ Keep America Beautiful-

The Bible passage I chose for today is
Psalm 95:4-5. Please, look it up and read it aloud to
the group.

Discuss how this Bible passage relates to today's
holiday.

Activity Suggestion:
1) Clean up the yard where you are staying or where
you have your group. Get rid of any trash. Do what
you can to have a nice looking yard.

What did you do today to observe this holiday?
Add any thoughts about your experience.

April 26
Worldwide Bereaved Spouses Awareness Month-

The Bible passage I chose for today is Psalm 68:5. Please, look it up and read it aloud to the group.

Discuss how this Bible passage relates to today's holiday.

Activity Suggestions:
1) Spend some time with someone who is lonely and missing that constant companionship they once had, be it from a spouse or another loved one.
2) If you cannot spend time with them, call or write them. Let them know you care.

What did you do today to observe this holiday? Add any thoughts about your experience.

April 27
Alcohol Awareness Month-

The Bible passage I chose for today is
Romans 13:13. Please, look it up and read it aloud
to the group.

Discuss how this Bible passage relates to today's
holiday.

Activity Suggestions:
1) Do you know someone who needs help? Please,
don't drink with them or enable their behavior.
Guide them towards getting the proper help, if you
can.
2) If alcohol is a problem in your life, please do not
hesitate to get the help you need.

What did you do today to observe this holiday?
Add any thoughts about your experience.

April 28
Morse Code Day-

The Bible passage I chose for today is
Proverbs 18:15. Please, look it up and read it aloud
to the group.

Discuss how this Bible passage relates to today's
holiday.

Activity Suggestion:
1) Get a copy of Morse Code for everyone in the
group. Have each person in the group tap out a
message in Morse Code, and everyone else try to
figure it out.

What did you do today to observe this holiday?
Add any thoughts about your experience.

April 29
International Dance Day-

The Bible passage I chose for today is
Psalm 30:11. Please, look it up and read it aloud to
the group.

Discuss how this Bible passage relates to today's
holiday.

Activity Suggestion:
1) Choose some appropriate music, learn some new
dance moves, and have fun.

What did you do today to observe this holiday?
Add any thoughts about your experience.

April 30
National Honesty Day-

The Bible passage I chose for today is
Leviticus 19:35-36. Please, look it up and read it
aloud to the group.

Discuss how this Bible passage relates to today's
holiday.

Activity Suggestion:
1) Honesty is more than not lying. Make sure all
your words and actions are honest. (Honesty is not
an excuse to be rude.)

What did you do today to observe this holiday?
Add any thoughts about your experience.

May 1
Posture Month-

The Bible passage I chose for today is
Psalm 100:3. Please, look it up and read it aloud to
the group.
*Note: I did not mistake posture for pasture. When you
know who you belong to, you can have the confidence to
stand straight and hold your head up high.*

Discuss how this Bible passage relates to today's
holiday.

Activity Suggestions:
1) Learn the importance of good posture.
2) Be aware of your posture all day. When you are
standing and walking today, imagine a string at the
top of your head pulling you up. When you are
sitting, don't slouch. Use a support behind your
lower back if you need one. Do not cross your legs
while sitting.

What did you do today to observe this holiday?
Add any thoughts about your experience.

May 2
Global Health and Fitness Month-

The Bible passage I chose for today is
1 Corinthians 6:19-20. Please, look it up and read it
aloud to the group.

Discuss how this Bible passage relates to today's
holiday.

Activity Suggestions:
1) If you have choices in food, make healthy
choices today.
2) Engage in some type of healthy physical activity
today.

What did you do today to observe this holiday?
Add any thoughts about your experience.

May 3
Better Sleep Month-

The Bible passage I chose for today is Psalm 4:8.
Please, look it up and read it aloud to the group.

Discuss how this Bible passage relates to today's
holiday.

Activity Suggestion:
1) Learn, and implement, healthy sleep habits.

What did you do today to observe this holiday?
Add any thoughts about your experience.

May 4
World Give Day-

The Bible passage I chose for today is
Matthew 5:16. Please, look it up and read it aloud to
the group.

Discuss how this Bible passage relates to today's
holiday.

Activity Suggestion:
1) Give of your time, and help someone with a task
that may be difficult or unpleasant for them.

What did you do today to observe this holiday?
Add any thoughts about your experience.

May 5
National Silence the Shame Day-

The Bible passages I chose for today are
1 Corinthians 6:9-11 and Philippians 4:8. Please,
look them up and read them aloud to the group.

Discuss how this Bible passage relates to today's
holiday.

Activity Suggestions:
1) Pray to God for forgiveness for past sins, and
then leave them there. Focus on the decisions you
are making today. Paul said "such were some of
you", not "such are some of you and you always
will be". Christ can change people. You can't be
the light in the world God wants you to be if you're
beating yourself up for past sins.
2) What if you sin again? Pray for forgiveness again.
Repent (turn from your sins) again. Never give up,
and never give up on yourself.
3) When you get thoughts that try to shame you for
a past you can't change, refer to Philippians 4:8.
Write it down and carry it with you, if it may be
helpful. If your thought isn't on that list, blink to
change the channel in your mind, or whatever you
can so to purposefully choose to think about
something that is worthy of that thinking list.
4) Do not do one thing you regret (like alcohol or
drugs) to try to forget about something else. That
will just make matters worse.

What did you do today to observe this holiday?
Add any thoughts about your experience.

May 6
Get Caught Reading Month-

The Bible passage I chose for today is
Philippians 4:8. Please, look it up and read it aloud
to the group.

Discuss how this Bible passage relates to today's
holiday.

Activity Suggestion:
1) Choose a good book to read today. Be sure that
it meets the criteria in the passage.

What did you do today to observe this holiday?
Add any thoughts about your experience.

May 7
Screen-Free Week/Digital Detox Week-

The Bible passage I chose for today is
1Timothy 6:6-8. Please, look it up and read it aloud
to the group.

Discuss how this Bible passage relates to today's
holiday.

Activity Suggestion:
1) Plan some screen-free activities for yourself and
your group. Challenge the group to see how long
they can go without any screen time (Which
includes using cell phones for anything except
phone calls).

What did you do today to observe this holiday?
Add any thoughts about your experience.

May 8
National Student Nurse Day-

The Bible passage I chose for today is 3 John 1:2.
Please, look it up and read it aloud to the group.

Discuss how this Bible passage relates to today's
holiday.

Activity Suggestions:
1) Thank all the nurses that help you. Be especially
patient and kind to student nurses.
2) Learn first aid and CPR if you can.

What did you do today to observe this holiday?
Add any thoughts about your experience.

May 9
Older Americans Month-

The Bible passage I chose for today is
Leviticus 19:32. Please, look it up and read it aloud
to the group.

Discuss how this Bible passage relates to today's
holiday.

Activity Suggestions:
1) Find time to spend with an elderly person. Let
them tell you their stories. They have a lot of
wisdom to share.
2) Maybe they just need someone to talk to. Be that
person for them. If you can't see them in person
right now, call or write.
3) Maybe they need a little help with something. Do
what you can to help out.

What did you do today to observe this holiday?
Add any thoughts about your experience.

May 10
National Smile Month-

The Bible passage I chose for today is
Proverbs 15:13. Please, look it up and read it aloud
to the group.

Discuss how this Bible passage relates to today's
holiday.

Activity Suggestion:
1) Make a concerted effort to make eye contact
with everyone you come into contact with (if they
look at you). When you make eye contact, smile.
Who knows? That smile may make a difference.

What did you do today to observe this holiday?
Add any thoughts about your experience.

May 11
World Ego Awareness Day-

The Bible passage I chose for today is
Romans 12:3. Please, look it up and read it aloud to
the group.

Discuss how this Bible passage relates to today's
holiday.

Activity Suggestions:
1) Be honest in determining if you think too highly
of yourself in certain areas. Do you expect others to
automatically defer to your opinion? Do you get
offended when others want a second opinion? Do
you get defensive when anyone offers a suggestion
or correction? What can you do to gain a more
honest view of yourself and display appropriate
confidence?
2) Do you have the opposite problem? Do you
have a hard time accepting a compliment? Are you
afraid to share your opinions? Do you always
assume the other person is right? What can you do
to gain a more honest view of yourself and display
appropriate confidence?
3) Maybe both apply in different situations and with
different people. Take the time to take an honest
look at yourself in this area.

What did you do today to observe this holiday?
Add any thoughts about your experience.

May 12
National Stuttering Awareness Week-

The Bible passage I chose for today is
Matthew 7:12. Please, look it up and read it aloud to
the group.

Discuss how this Bible passage relates to today's
holiday.

Activity Suggestions:
1) Learn a little about stuttering, and how to best be
supportive to people who stutter.
2) Do not make fun of anyone for how they speak-
stuttering, accent, voice, etc.
3) Discourage others from making fun of people.
Do so in a respectful way. Do not insult one person
for insulting another person.

What did you do today to observe this holiday?
Add any thoughts about your experience.

May 13
Tulip Day-

The Bible passage I chose for today is
Ecclesiastes 3:11. Please, look it up and read it
aloud to the group.

Discuss how this Bible passage relates to today's
holiday.

Activity Suggestions:
1) Go for a walk and enjoy the beautiful flowers,
and think about the wonders of God's creation.
2) Make a drawing, painting, or arts and crafts of
any kind involving tulips. You may choose to keep
your creation or bless someone else with it.

What did you do today to observe this holiday?
Add any thoughts about your experience.

May 14
The Stars and Stripes Forever Day-

The Bible passage I chose for today is
Psalm 46:10. Please, look it up and read it aloud to
the group.

Discuss how this Bible passage relates to today's
holiday.

Activity Suggestions:
1) Sing some patriotic songs that reference God.
2) Learn a little about the role faith in God played
in the founding of this country.

What did you do today to observe this holiday?
Add any thoughts about your experience.

May 15
International Day of Families -

 The Bible passage I chose for today is
Psalm 133:1. Please, look it up and read it aloud to
the group.

Discuss how this Bible passage relates to today's
holiday.

Activity Suggestions:
1) Do what you can to make peace with any family
member with whom there is any conflict.
2) Write a letter or call a family member that you
haven't contacted in awhile.

What did you do today to observe this holiday?
Add any thoughts about your experience.

May 16
Love a Tree Day-

The Bible passage I chose for today is Micah 4:4.
Please, look it up and read it aloud to the group.

Discuss how this Bible passage relates to today's
holiday.

Activity Suggestions:
1) Find a tree to sit under and enjoy some peace in
the shade.
2) Make a painting (or any type of art) of a
landscape with a tree or trees of your choice. As
always, you could choose to keep your art or bless
someone else with it.

What did you do today to observe this holiday?
Add any thoughts about your experience.

May 17
World Hypertension Day-

The Bible passage I chose for today is
Proverbs 17:22. Please, look it up and read it aloud
to the group.

Discuss how this Bible passage relates to today's
holiday.

Activity Suggestion:
1) Learn a little about hypertension, and then get
your blood pressure checked. Some places have
free stations that check your blood pressure. If it is
high or too low, learn ways to improve it, and/or
seek medical attention if needed.

What did you do today to observe this holiday?
Add any thoughts about your experience.

May 18
Visit Your Relatives Day-

The Bible passage I chose for today is
Ecclesiastes 4:9-12. Please, look it up and read it
aloud to the group.

Discuss how this Bible passage relates to today's
holiday.

Activity Suggestions:
1) If you are able, visit a relative you haven't seen in
awhile, or who may be lonely.
2) If you cannot visit them, invite them to visit you.
3) If you can do neither of the above, call or write
them.

What did you do today to observe this holiday?
Add any thoughts about your experience.

May 19
Celebrate Your Elected Officials Day-

The Bible passage I chose for today is
Proverbs 29:14. Please, look it up and read it aloud
to the group.

Discuss how this Bible passage relates to today's
holiday.

Activity Suggestions:
1) Post on social media something good that an
elected official has done.
2) Write a letter or email to an elected official
thanking them for their position on a certain policy.
3) If you do not know anything positive about any
elected officials, look up their stances on important
issues.

What did you do today to observe this holiday?
Add any thoughts about your experience.

May 20
Food Allergy Action Month-

The Bible passage I chose for today is
Philippians 2:4. Please, look it up and read it aloud
to the group.

Discuss how this Bible passage relates to today's
holiday.

Activity Suggestions:
1) Learn about food allergies, and share that
knowledge on social media (if you are on social
media), or with others if you have the opportunity.
2) Be thoughtful to those that have food allergies. If
you have a gathering, be mindful of the food
offered.

What did you do today to observe this holiday?
Add any thoughts about your experience.

May 21
World Day for Cultural Diversity for Dialogue
& Development-

The Bible passage I chose for today is
Matthew 28:19-20. Please, look it up and read it
aloud to the group.

Discuss how this Bible passage relates to today's
holiday.

Activity Suggestions:
1) Learn about the religious persecution that still
goes on in some countries, and to some degree,
even in our own. Discuss things you can do to help
end religious persecution.
2) Share awareness about religious persecution that
still exists.
3) Share your faith with someone from another
culture. You may consider inviting them to this
group.

What did you do today to observe this holiday?
Add any thoughts about your experience.

May 22
National Solitaire Day-

The Bible passage I chose for today is Mark 6:31.
Please, look it up and read it aloud to the group.

Discuss how this Bible passage relates to today's
holiday.

Activity Suggestions:
1) Get a deck of cards and teach the group how to
play solitaire (for those who do not already know).
This is a simple, inexpensive game that can provide
a relief from boredom, give a person a distraction
from unpleasant thoughts, etc.
2) This game can also be played online. It is
probably healthier to use a deck of cards, though,
so there isn't screen time involved.

What did you do today to observe this holiday?
Add any thoughts about your experience.

May 23
Motorcycle Safety Month-

The Bible passage I chose for today is
Galatians 5:14. Please, look it up and read it aloud
to the group.

Discuss how this Bible passage relates to today's
holiday.

Activity Suggestions:
1) Learn about motorcycle safety, as there are some
actions taken by motorcycle drivers for safety that
get misinterpreted by others.
2) If you drive a motorcycle, wear a helmet and
follow all safe driving practices.
3) If you drive anything else, be considerate to
motorcycle drivers that you encounter on the road.

What did you do today to observe this holiday?
Add any thoughts about your experience.

May 24
Culture and Literacy Day (Bulgaria)-

The Bible passage I chose for today is
Leviticus 19:34. Please, look it up and read it aloud
to the group.

Discuss how this Bible passage relates to today's
holiday.

Activity Suggestion:
1) Read a little about a culture (not religion) other
than your own. You may choose Bulgaria, as this is
where the holiday seems to have originated.
However, choose any country and culture you wish.
We are often kinder when we have some
understanding of those who are different.

What did you do today to observe this holiday?
Add any thoughts about your experience.

May 25
National Missing Children's Day-

The Bible passage I chose for today is
Matthew 18:10. Please, look it up and read it aloud
to the group.

Discuss how this Bible passage relates to today's
holiday.

Activity Suggestions:
1) Take the time to look at the flyers for missing
children on the notification boards in stores,
instead of just walking by.
2) Look up a site for missing children, and share
some of the children's pictures on social media.
You never know if one of your contacts may have
seen them.
3) If you have any information on the abduction or
captivity of anyone, please inform authorities. You
can do so anonymously, but please report what you
know. If it is just a suspicion, and you are not
absolutely sure, report it as such. You could be
right, and it could save a life or save someone from
lots of trauma.

What did you do today to observe this holiday?
Add any thoughts about your experience.

May 26
Mental Health Month-

The Bible passage I chose for today is Jonah 2:4-7.
Please, look it up and read it aloud to the group.

Discuss how this Bible passage relates to today's
holiday.

Activity Suggestions:
1) Spend some time with someone who may be
going through some emotional challenges, and try
to learn a little about what they are going through.
2) If that person is you, find a trusted friend you
can talk to, or seek professional help. Give yourself
a break, and know that you are not alone. Pray to
God for guidance, healing, peace, and whatever it is
that you need.

What did you do today to observe this holiday?
Add any thoughts about your experience.

May 27
Nothing to Fear Day-

The Bible passage I chose for today is Joshua 1:9.
Please, look it up and read it aloud to the group.

Discuss how this Bible passage relates to today's
holiday.

Activity Suggestions:
1) Pray to God about all that is troubling you.
2) Journal about your fears.
3) Learn some relaxation techniques, especially for
your breathing and tight muscles, so that you can
help control your physical response to fear.

What did you do today to observe this holiday?
Add any thoughts about your experience.

May 28
Whooping Crane Day-

The Bible passage I chose for today is Genesis 1:20.
Please, look it up and read it aloud to the group.

Discuss how this Bible passage relates to today's
holiday.

Activity Suggestions:
1) Watch a video together about the whooping
crane.
2) Make a drawing or painting of the whooping
crane in its natural habitat (on the ground or flying).
As always, you may choose to keep your art or bless
someone else with it.

What did you do today to observe this holiday?
Add any thoughts about your experience.

May 29
National Backyard Games Week (week before Memorial Day)-

The Bible passage I chose for today is 2 Timothy 2:5. Please, look it up and read it aloud to the group.

Discuss how this Bible passage relates to today's holiday.

Activity Suggestion:
1) Spend time playing games outside with the group. Play by the rules. Remember good sportsmanship. The games you choose do not matter. It is the time spent together getting some fresh air that matters.

What did you do today to observe this holiday? Add any thoughts about your experience.

May 30
National Family Month (between Mother's Day and Father's Day)-

The Bible passage I chose for today is
Ephesians 6:1-4. Please, look it up and read it aloud
to the group.

Discuss how this Bible passage relates to today's
holiday.

Activity Suggestion:
1) If you cannot see your family today, call or write
them. Contact as many family members today as
you can, especially those you may have lost touch
with.

What did you do today to observe this holiday?
Add any thoughts about your experience.

May 31
What You Think upon Grows Day-

The Bible passage I chose for today is
Philippians 4:8. Please, look it up and read it aloud
to the group.

Discuss how this Bible passage relates to today's
holiday.

Activity Suggestions:
1) Write out Philippians 4:8, or make an artistic
drawing or painting with the words listed, as a
thought list reminder.
2) Use Philippians 4:8 to monitor your thoughts
today.

What did you do today to observe this holiday?
Add any thoughts about your experience.

7

JUNE

June 1
Heimlich Maneuver Day-

The Bible passage I chose for today is Luke 6:9.
Please, look it up and read it aloud to the group.

Discuss how this Bible passage relates to today's
holiday.

Activity Suggestion:
1) Learn (or review) how and when to do the
Heimlich Maneuver.

What did you do today to observe this holiday?
Add any thoughts about your experience.

June 2
American Indian Citizenship Day-

The Bible passage I chose for today is
Hebrews 12:14. Please, look it up and read it aloud
to the group.

Discuss how this Bible passage relates to today's
holiday.

Activity Suggestion:
1) Learn a little about the history of American
Indians, and when they became citizens of the
United States. Also, become informed of some
issues that still exist for those living on reservations.

What did you do today to observe this holiday?
Add any thoughts about your experience.

June 3
PTSD Awareness Month-

The Bible passage I chose for today is Isaiah 61:1-3.
Please, look it up and read it aloud to the group.

Discuss how this Bible passage relates to today's
holiday.

Activity Suggestion:
1) Learn what you can about PTSD, and share that
knowledge on social media, and/or with other
people in your life in person.

What did you do today to observe this holiday?
Add any thoughts about your experience.

June 4
Gun Violence Awareness Day-

The Bible passage I chose for today is
Proverbs 11:14. Please, look it up and read it aloud
to the group.

Discuss how this Bible passage relates to today's
holiday.

Activity Suggestion:
1) Discuss gun violence issues with your group. Be
sure to listen as much as you talk.

What did you do today to observe this holiday?
Add any thoughts about your experience.

June 5
World Environment Day-

The Bible passage I chose for today is Genesis 2:15.
Please, look it up and read it aloud to the group.

Discuss how this Bible passage relates to today's
holiday.

Activity Suggestions:
1) Go to a local park, and pick up trash. Wear
gloves and take precautions, such as not touching
anything questionable. If you find anything
dangerous, call the police so they can safely remove
it.
2) If you cannot go to a park, clean up the outside
of where you are.
3) Learn about recycling and brainstorm other
things that you can personally do to help the
environment.

What did you do today to observe this holiday?
Add any thoughts about your experience.

June 6
National Yo-Yo Day-

The Bible passage I chose for today is Mark 6:31.
Please, look it up and read it aloud to the group.

Discuss how this Bible passage relates to today's
holiday.

Activity Suggestion:
1) Learn (or relearn) how to use a yo-yo. You may
even want to learn some tricks. This is a simple
form of relaxation that can help distract your mind
from unwanted thoughts.

What did you do today to observe this holiday?
Add any thoughts about your experience.

June 7
Effective Communications Month-

The Bible passage I chose for today is
Proverbs 18:13. Please, look it up and read it aloud
to the group.

Discuss how this Bible passage relates to today's
holiday.

Activity Suggestion:
1) Make sure that your communications are clear,
that you understand the other people, and that they
understand you. Also, make sure that whatever you
say is honest, with no deceit.

What did you do today to observe this holiday?
Add any thoughts about your experience.

June 8
Best Friends Day-

The Bible passage I chose for today is
Proverbs 18:24. Please, look it up and read it aloud
to the group.

Discuss how this Bible passage relates to today's
holiday.

Activity Suggestion:
1) Determine who really is your best friend, and
write or call that person today.

What did you do today to observe this holiday?
Add any thoughts about your experience.

June 9
Safety Month-

The Bible passage I chose for today is
Ecclesiastes 7:12. Please, look it up and read it
aloud to the group.

Discuss how this Bible passage relates to today's
holiday.

Activity Suggestions:
1) Look for safety hazards around you, and do what
you can to correct them.
2) Take the appropriate safety precautions when
you do things. You can have fun while staying safe.

What did you do today to observe this holiday?
Add any thoughts about your experience.

June 10
Great Outdoors Month-

The Bible passage I chose for today is Job 12:7-10. Please, look it up and read it aloud to the group.

Discuss how this Bible passage relates to today's holiday.

Activity Suggestion:
1) Spend some time outdoors today, enjoying God's creation.

What did you do today to observe this holiday? Add any thoughts about your experience.

June 11
National Making Life Beautiful Day-

The Bible passage I chose for today is 1 Peter 4:9.
Please, look it up and read it aloud to the group.

Discuss how this Bible passage relates to today's
holiday.

Activity Suggestion:
1) Do something today to make someone's day a
little better. It can be anyone, even a complete
stranger. In fact, kindness from a stranger can be
especially uplifting.

What did you do today to observe this holiday?
Add any thoughts about your experience.

June 12
Rebuild Your Life Month-

The Bible passage I chose for today is James 1:5.
Please, look it up and read it aloud to the group.

Discuss how this Bible passage relates to today's
holiday.

Activity Suggestion:
1) Think of an area of your life that you want to
change. Then, pray for God to give you the
wisdom, strength, and whatever you need to work
towards those changes.

What did you do today to observe this holiday?
Add any thoughts about your experience.

June 13
Write to Your Father Day-

The Bible passage I chose for today is
Exodus 20:12. Please, look it up and read it aloud
to the group.

Discuss how this Bible passage relates to today's
holiday.

Activity Suggestion:
1) Write a letter to your father. If he is no longer
living, write a tribute to him.

What did you do today to observe this holiday?
Add any thoughts about your experience.

June 14
World Blood Donor Day-

The Bible passage I chose for today is John 15:13.
Please, look it up and read it aloud to the group.
*Note: You aren't giving your life, but you are giving of
yourself to give life to someone else.*

Discuss how this Bible passage relates to today's
holiday.

Activity Suggestions:
1) Make an appointment to donate blood.
2) If you cannot donate blood, consider being an
organ donor. Make sure that you are not only
registered as an organ donor on your driver's
license, but that your family knows your wishes, so
that they don't try to stop it when the time comes.

What did you do today to observe this holiday?
Add any thoughts about your experience.

June 15
World Elder Abuse Awareness Day-

The Bible passage I chose for today is
Leviticus 19:32. Please, look it up and read it aloud
to the group.

Discuss how this Bible passage relates to today's
holiday.

Activity Suggestions:
1) Be kind to any elderly people in your life,
including strangers on the street or in the stores
that you can greet and possibly help.
2) If you know someone being abused, please
report it. If it is not to the level of being reportable,
try to ease some of the pressure from the caregiver,
or otherwise do what you can to improve the
situation.
3) Keep in regular contact with the elderly people in
your life, especially your relatives.
4) If you are being abused, tell someone you can
trust to help you and/or report it to the proper
authorities.

What did you do today to observe this holiday?
Add any thoughts about your experience.

June 16
Wish Fulfillment Day-

The Bible passage I chose for today is
1 Corinthians 10:24. Please, look it up and read it
aloud to the group.

Discuss how this Bible passage relates to today's
holiday.

Activity Suggestion:
1) Do what you can to make a wish of someone
else come true (no matter how small).

What did you do today to observe this holiday?
Add any thoughts about your experience.

June 17
Eat Your Vegetables Day-

The Bible passage I chose for today is
Daniel 1:12-13. Please, look it up and read it aloud
to the group.

Discuss how this Bible passage relates to today's
holiday.

Activity Suggestions:
1) Eat your vegetables today.
2) If you have an opportunity, try a new recipe that
includes vegetables.
3) Try a vegetable that you have been afraid to try
before, or in a new way.

What did you do today to observe this holiday?
Add any thoughts about your experience.

June 18
Autistic Pride Day-

The Bible passage I chose for today is
Romans 12:4-9. Please, look it up and read it aloud
to the group.

Discuss how this Bible passage relates to today's
holiday.

Activity Suggestions:
1) Learn about autism and neurodiversity.
2) Watch a video of people with autism discussing
their abilities and feelings about having autism.

What did you do today to observe this holiday?
Add any thoughts about your experience.

June 19
World Sauntering Day-

The Bible passage I chose for today is
Philippians 4:6-7. Please, look it up and read it
aloud to the group.

Discuss how this Bible passage relates to today's
holiday.

Activity Suggestions:
1) Schedule in some quiet time today to pray.
2) You may want to go for a leisurely walk to enjoy
God's creation. Take the time to listen to the birds
and enjoy the beauty of the trees and flowers.
3) Enjoy the sunrise and/or sunset.
4) Take the time to breathe and relax.

What did you do today to observe this holiday?
Add any thoughts about your experience.

June 20
World Productivity Day-

The Bible passage I chose for today is
Ephesians 5:15-16. Please, look it up and read it
aloud to the group.

Discuss how this Bible passage relates to today's
holiday.

Activity Suggestion:
1) Think of one time waster to eliminate, or one
way to be more productive in your day, and then
implement your plan.

What did you do today to observe this holiday?
Add any thoughts about your experience.

June 21
World Music Day-

The Bible passage I chose for today is
Psalm 98:4-6. Please, look it up and read it aloud to
the group.

Discuss how this Bible passage relates to today's
holiday.

Activity Suggestions:
1) Choose some Christian, or otherwise clean and
decent music, and dance, or simply enjoy the music
and your day.
2) If you play an instrument, this would be a good
day to practice...alone or with others.
3) You could also get creative and use common
objects as musical instruments and have fun singing
and playing your new improvised instruments.

What did you do today to observe this holiday?
Add any thoughts about your experience.

June 22
World Rainforest Day-

The Bible passage I chose for today is
Job 12:7-10. Please, look it up and read it aloud to
the group.

Discuss how this Bible passage relates to today's
holiday.

Activity Suggestions:
1) Learn about rainforests. Look at pictures of
various ones.
2) Paint or draw a picture of a rainforest. As always,
you may choose to keep your art or bless someone
else with it.

What did you do today to observe this holiday?
Add any thoughts about your experience.

June 23
Let It Go Day-

The Bible passage I chose for today is
Ephesians 4:31-32. Please, look it up and read it
aloud to the group.

Discuss how this Bible passage relates to today's
holiday.

Activity Suggestion:
1) Is there something that keeps coming back into
your mind, causing you to feel upset, someone that
wronged you, something that keeps you up at night,
etc.? Find a way to think about it differently (or at
least put it in its place) and let it go. This could take
some time in prayer, journaling, determined
practice, etc. but it will be well worth it to regain
your peace.

What did you do today to observe this holiday?
Add any thoughts about your experience.

June 24
Celebration of the Senses-

The Bible passage I chose for today is
Psalm 115:1-9. Please, look it up and read it aloud
to the group.

Discuss how this Bible passage relates to today's
holiday.

Activity Suggestion:
1) Think of your blessings throughout the day,
thanking God for them. Try to think of God's
blessings that you experience from all of your
senses, such as the tasty food to eat, the smell of
fresh bread, hugging a loved one, etc.

What did you do today to observe this holiday?
Add any thoughts about your experience.

June 25
School Prayer Banned Anniversary-

The Bible passage I chose for today is
1 Thessalonians 5:17. Please, look it up and read it
aloud to the group.

Discuss how this Bible passage relates to today's
holiday.

Activity Suggestions:
1) Learn what this ban does and does not entail.
2) Find a way to support Christian groups and/or
individuals in public schools.
3) Do not let where you are or who you are with
stop you from praying. You can pray silently,
quietly, or aloud. You can pray alone, with someone
else, or with a group. Do whatever seems
appropriate at the time.

What did you do today to observe this holiday?
Add any thoughts about your experience.

June 26
Forgiveness Day-

The Bible passage I chose for today is
Matthew 6:14. Please, look it up and read it aloud to
the group.

Discuss how this Bible passage relates to today's
holiday.

Activity Suggestion:
1) Pray for the people that you feel have recently
wronged you. Pray for them to find God if they are
non-believers. Pray for peace and happiness for
them. Depending on the situation, pray for repaired
relationships with others you know they are
struggling with, healing from medical conditions, or
whatever would help them.

What did you do today to observe this holiday?
Add any thoughts about your experience.

June 27
Celibacy Awareness Month/ Decide to Be Married Day-

The Bible passage I chose for today is
1 Corinthians 7:8-9. Please, look it up and read it
aloud to the group.

Discuss how this Bible passage relates to today's
holiday.

Activity Suggestions:
1) Whether you are single or married, celebrate that
today.
2) If you are having sex outside of marriage, please
spend some time praying, reading the Bible to learn
what God wants, and make the necessary changes
in your life to follow God's will.

What did you do today to observe this holiday?
Add any thoughts about your experience.

June 28
Insurance Awareness Day-

The Bible passage I chose for today is Job 12:7-10.
Please, look it up and read it aloud to the group.

Discuss how this Bible passage relates to today's
holiday.

Activity Suggestion:
1) Learn about the different types of insurance that
there are. Which ones are mandatory and which are
voluntary? Look into the prices and the coverage,
and think about what would be right for you and
your family.

What did you do today to observe this holiday?
Add any thoughts about your experience.

June 29
National Rose Month-

The Bible passage I chose for today is
1 Thessalonians 5:11. Please, look it up and read it
aloud to the group.

Discuss how this Bible passage relates to today's
holiday.

Activity Suggestion:
1) Give a rose to someone who is special to you.
This does not need to be romantic. This could be
with love and appreciation to Mom, Grandma, an
aunt, a nice neighbor, etc. This could also be a live
rose, or one that you made in some form of craft,
or even a drawing or painting.

What did you do today to observe this holiday?
Add any thoughts about your experience.

June 30
Social Media Day-

The Bible passage I chose for today is
Philippians 4:8. Please, look it up and read it aloud
to the group.

Discuss how this Bible passage relates to today's
holiday.

Activity Suggestion:
1) Go through your social media, and make sure
every post you have created or shared meets the
criteria of today's Bible verse. Delete those that do
not meet this standard. Hide those in your news
feed that violate this standard.

What did you do today to observe this holiday?
Add any thoughts about your experience.

8

JULY

July 1
Social Wellness Month-

The Bible passage I chose for today is Psalm 1:1.
Please, look it up and read it aloud to the group.

Discuss how this Bible passage relates to today's
holiday.

Activity Suggestion:
1) Think about the people you spend time with. Are
there people who influence you in a negative way?
If you cannot be the positive influence, and they are
influencing you in a negative way, then consider
distancing yourself from them for your own sake,
and for the sake of those who look to you as an
example.

What did you do today to observe this holiday?
Add any thoughts about your experience.

July 2
I Forgot Day-

The Bible passage I chose for today is
Ecclesiastes 5:5. Please, look it up and read it aloud
to the group.

Discuss how this Bible passage relates to today's
holiday.

Activity Suggestion:
1) What can you do to purposefully remember your
obligations? If you have a smart phone, you can
program important dates into your calendar, as well
as setting timers. You can use a wall calendar, day
planner, and sticky notes to remember things as
well. Take the time to write down reminders, so you
don't forget things that are important to you and
others.

What did you do today to observe this holiday?
Add any thoughts about your experience.

July 3
Eye Injury Prevention Month-

The Bible passage I chose for today is
Ephesians 5:15. Please, look it up and read it aloud
to the group.

Discuss how this Bible passage relates to today's
holiday.

Activity Suggestions:
1) Learn a little about eye safety, and take
appropriate precautions when it is wise to do so.
2) If you engage in any activities where wearing eye
protection is advised, be sure that you have a good
pair of safety glasses, and use them when
appropriate.

What did you do today to observe this holiday?
Add any thoughts about your experience.

July 4
Invisible Day-

The Bible passage I chose for today is Galatians 6:9.
Please, look it up and read it aloud to the group.

Discuss how this Bible passage relates to today's
holiday.

Activity Suggestion:
1) Discuss what you would do if you were invisible
for a day, and why. Be as detailed as you can.

What did you do today to observe this holiday?
Add any thoughts about your experience.

July 5
Anti-Boredom Month-

The Bible passage I chose for today is 1 Peter 5:8.
Please, look it up and read it aloud to the group.

Discuss how this Bible passage relates to today's
holiday.

Activity Suggestion:
1) Make a list of as many positive things as you can
to do when you feel bored. Keep this list. Be
prepared for those times, so that you do not
become tempted to do the wrong things.

What did you do today to observe this holiday?
Add any thoughts about your experience.

July 6
Self-Care Month-

The Bible passage I chose for today is 3 John 1:2.
Please, look it up and read it aloud to the group.

Discuss how this Bible passage relates to today's
holiday.

Activity Suggestion:
1) Make a list of many things you can do to keep
yourself physically, mentally, emotionally, and
spiritually healthy. Keep this list as a reminder to do
them when needed.

What did you do today to observe this holiday?
Add any thoughts about your experience.

July 7
Tell the Truth Day-

The Bible passage I chose for today is
Ephesians 4:25. Please, look it up and read it aloud
to the group.

Discuss how this Bible passage relates to today's
holiday.

Activity Suggestion:
1) Be honest at all times, but do not use honesty as
an excuse to be rude and disrespectful. Not every
thought needs to be said aloud.

What did you do today to observe this holiday?
Add any thoughts about your experience.

July 8
Be a Kid Again Day-

The Bible passage I chose for today is Luke 18:17. Please, look it up and read it aloud to the group.

Discuss how this Bible passage relates to today's holiday.

Activity Suggestions:
1) What were some good parts about childhood? What did you like better about yourself then? What are some things that are better now? What do you like better about yourself now?
2) Think of something that you enjoyed as a child that you can do today. (Make sure it is appropriate.)

What did you do today to observe this holiday? Add any thoughts about your experience.

July 9
National Don't Put All Your Eggs in One Omelet Day-

The Bible passage I chose for today is
James 4:13-17. Please, look it up and read it aloud
to the group.

Discuss how this Bible passage relates to today's
holiday.

Activity Suggestion:
1) When you make plans, give yourself some
options. Be prepared for things to not go exactly as
planned.

What did you do today to observe this holiday?
Add any thoughts about your experience.

July 10
Cell Phone Courtesy Month-

The Bible passage I chose for today is Luke 6:31.
Please, look it up and read it aloud to the group.

Discuss how this Bible passage relates to today's
holiday.

Activity Suggestions:
1) Look up some cell phone etiquette tips, and
figure out ways you could be more polite to others
with the use of your cell phone (if you have one).
2) If you do not have a cell phone, look up some
general etiquette tips for social situations.

What did you do today to observe this holiday?
Add any thoughts about your experience.

July 11
Cheer Up the Lonely Day-

The Bible passage I chose for today is
Proverbs 18:24. Please, look it up and read it aloud
to the group.

Discuss how this Bible passage relates to today's
holiday.

Activity Suggestions:
1) Take some time to spend with someone who
could use the company.
2) If you cannot visit in person, call or write them.

What did you do today to observe this holiday?
Add any thoughts about your experience.

July 12
Simplicity Day-

The Bible passage I chose for today is
1 Timothy 6:6-7. Please, look it up and read it aloud
to the group.

Discuss how this Bible passage relates to today's
holiday.

Activity Suggestions:
1) Keep things simple today. Try to think of one
thing you could do in a simpler way.
2) Evaluate your priorities, and the value of the
things in your life.

What did you do today to observe this holiday?
Add any thoughts about your experience.

July 13
Barbershop Music Appreciation Day-

The Bible passage I chose for today is
Proverbs 17:22. Please, look it up and read it aloud
to the group.

Discuss how this Bible passage relates to today's
holiday.

Activity Suggestion:
1) Listen to some barbershop music today.

What did you do today to observe this holiday?
Add any thoughts about your experience.

July 14
Pandemonium Day-

The Bible passage I chose for today is John 14:27.
Please, look it up and read it aloud to the group.

Discuss how this Bible passage relates to today's
holiday.

Activity Suggestion:
1) What do you do when things do not go as
planned? How do you handle the chaos? How can
you prepare to handle those situations in a more
positive way?

What did you do today to observe this holiday?
Add any thoughts about your experience.

July 15
Wild about Wildlife Month-

The Bible passage I chose for today is Isaiah 11:6-9.
Please, look it up and read it aloud to the group.

Discuss how this Bible passage relates to today's
holiday.

Activity Suggestions:
1) Watch a wildlife video.
2) Make a drawing or painting of your favorite
wildlife animal in its natural habitat. As always, you
may choose to keep your art or bless someone else
with it.

What did you do today to observe this holiday?
Add any thoughts about your experience.

July 16
Sports Cliché Week-

The Bible passage I chose for today is
Philippians 4:13. Please, look it up and read it aloud
to the group.

Discuss how this Bible passage relates to today's
holiday.

Activity Suggestion:
1) Think of a few sports clichés. Then, find a
meaningful Bible verse that can help you or others
with your physical fitness goals. The one I chose
for this day is listed above. It does not just apply to
physical goals, but could be applied generally to
challenges you face.

What did you do today to observe this holiday?
Add any thoughts about your experience.

July 17
World Day for International Criminal Justice-

The Bible passage I chose for today is Isaiah 1:17.
Please, look it up and read it aloud to the group.

Discuss how this Bible passage relates to today's
holiday.

Activity Suggestion:
1) Learn about issues in other countries as well as
your own. Care about all people, not just those
around you.

What did you do today to observe this holiday?
Add any thoughts about your experience.

July 18
World Listening Day-

The Bible passage I chose for today is James 1:19.
Please, look it up and read it aloud to the group.

Discuss how this Bible passage relates to today's
holiday.

Activity Suggestion:
1) Ask someone their opinion about something
today, and truly listen to their answer. Don't think
about your side of the argument or what you are
going to say next. Just focus on understanding what
the person is trying to say. Then, after thoughtful
consideration, respond appropriately.

What did you do today to observe this holiday?
Add any thoughts about your experience.

July 19
New Friends Day-

The Bible passage I chose for today is
Psalm 133:1. Please, look it up and read it aloud to
the group.

Discuss how this Bible passage relates to today's
holiday.

Activity Suggestions:
1) Strike up a conversation with someone you do
not know, or do not know well.
2) Sit by someone different than you normally do in
group, lunch, etc.

What did you do today to observe this holiday?
Add any thoughts about your experience.

July 20
Jesus' Birthday Observed (Christmas in July)-

The Bible passage I chose for today is
Deuteronomy 12:29-32. Please, look it up and read
it aloud to the group.

*Note: (I do encourage you to do your own investigating into
these matters, if you wish). From what I have found, there is
no agreement as to when Jesus was born, but December 25th
is unlikely. Instead, that tradition may have started with the
Catholic church tying in winter solstice and Saturnalia with
Jesus' birthday (Castro & Leggett, 2021). It may have also
started with Constantine blending pagan and Christian
holidays, as that date is believed to have been used previously
to celebrate the sun god's birthday (Geller, 2016). Also,
Christmas has become very commercialized and more secular
than Christian. It seems that most songs with the word
Christmas in them are not even about Jesus. So, to avoid
religious syncretism, to guess at a day more likely to be close
to the correct time of His birth, and to play with the
Christmas in July idea, this is the day I will use as the day
to observe Jesus' birthday. St. Nicholas will get his day on
the day already appointed to him. Don't be surprised, but
that's not December 25th, either. It is already documented as
being December 6th (Henry, 2020), which is great, because
then the sun god's birthday is not celebrated with any of that.*

Discuss how this Bible passage relates to today's
holiday.

Activity Suggestions:
1) Celebrate Jesus' birthday by reading stories of
His birth and His life.
2) Honor Jesus by doing something to help
someone in need.
3) Listen to Christmas songs that are about Jesus.

What did you do today to observe this holiday?
Add any thoughts about your experience.

July 21
No Pet Store Puppies Day-

The Bible passage I chose for today is Job 12:7-10. Please, look it up and read it aloud to the group.

Discuss how this Bible passage relates to today's holiday.

Activity Suggestion:
1) Learn about the negative effects of buying pet store puppies as opposed to adopting those in shelters, and then share that information with others in person and/or on social media.

What did you do today to observe this holiday? Add any thoughts about your experience.

July 22
Summer Leisure Day-

The Bible passage I chose for today is
Ecclesiastes 4:9-12. Please, look it up and read it
aloud to the group.

Discuss how this Bible passage relates to today's
holiday.

Activity Suggestion:
1) Spend some time today relaxing and enjoying life
with someone who has been there for you.

What did you do today to observe this holiday?
Add any thoughts about your experience.

July 23
Refreshment Day-

The Bible passage I chose for today is
Proverbs 16:24. Please, look it up and read it aloud
to the group.

Discuss how this Bible passage relates to today's
holiday.

Activity Suggestion:
1) Make a pitcher of lemonade for your group.
Spend some time encouraging each other in
whatever is important to each of you.

What did you do today to observe this holiday?
Add any thoughts about your experience.

July 24
Tell an Old Joke Day-

The Bible passage I chose for today is
Proverbs 17:22. Please, look it up and read it aloud
to the group.

Discuss how this Bible passage relates to today's
holiday.

Activity Suggestion:
1) Take turns telling old jokes. Make sure they are
appropriate.

What did you do today to observe this holiday?
Add any thoughts about your experience.

July 25
Video Games Day-

The Bible passage I chose for today is
Ephesians 4:31. Please, look it up and read it aloud
to the group.

Discuss how this Bible passage relates to today's
holiday.

Activity Suggestion:
1) Use the following verse, as well as others that
you know, and use a Christian standard to sort
through all of the video games that you play or that
you have in your home. Do not play or house those
that you know would not be approved by God.

What did you do today to observe this holiday?
Add any thoughts about your experience.

July 26
Americans with Disabilities Day-

The Bible passage I chose for today is
Luke 14:13. Please, look it up and read it aloud to
the group.

Discuss how these Bible passages relate to today's
holiday.

Activity Suggestion:
1) Today, spend time thinking about the different
types of disabilities there are, and your attitudes
towards people who are living with those
conditions. If you have a disability, think about
your attitudes towards people without your
disability, or those who have a different condition.
Sometimes, simple awareness of one's feelings and
thoughts is enough to generate change.

What did you do today to observe this holiday?
Add any thoughts about your experience.

July 27
Love is Kind-

The Bible passage I chose for today is
Galatians 5:22-23. Please, look it up and read it
aloud to the group.

Discuss how this Bible passage relates to today's
holiday.

Activity Suggestion:
1) What can you do to show love towards God's
creation? This could be towards a person, animal,
habitat, etc.

What did you do today to observe this holiday?
Add any thoughts about your experience.

July 28
Outdoor Month-

The Bible passage I chose for today is Isaiah 55:12.
Please, look it up and read it aloud to the group.

Discuss how this Bible passage relates to today's
holiday.

Activity Suggestions:
1) Spend some time today outdoors, enjoying
nature.
2) Spend some time playing outdoor games.

What did you do today to observe this holiday?
Add any thoughts about your experience.

July 29
Rain Day-

The Bible passage I chose for today is
Isaiah 55:10-11. Please, look it up and read it aloud
to the group.

Discuss how this Bible passage relates to today's
holiday.

Activity Suggestions:
1) If it happens to be raining, enjoy watching it and
listening to it.
2) Instead of focusing on what you cannot do on a
rainy day, brainstorm positive things that you can
do.
3) Make a list of all the good things about rain.

What did you do today to observe this holiday?
Add any thoughts about your experience.

July 30
Friendship Day-

The Bible passage I chose for today is
Proverbs 20:6. Please, look it up and read it aloud
to the group.

Discuss how this Bible passage relates to today's
holiday.

Activity Suggestions:
1) Spend some time with a friend today.
2) If you can't visit, then call or text and let them
know you are thinking of them.

What did you do today to observe this holiday?
Add any thoughts about your experience.

July 31
Uncommon Instruments Awareness Day-

The Bible passage I chose for today is
Psalm 150:1-6. Please, look it up and read it aloud
to the group.

Discuss how this Bible passage relates to today's
holiday.

Activity Suggestions:
1) Spend some time today learning about unusual
instruments, and listening to some, if possible.
2) Use some common household items as
instruments, and sing and play a song together as a
group.

What did you do today to observe this holiday?
Add any thoughts about your experience.

9
AUGUST

August 1
Respect for Parents Day-

The Bible passage I chose for today is
Ephesians 6:2. Please, look it up and read it aloud
to the group.

Discuss how this Bible passage relates to today's
holiday.

Activity Suggestions:
1) Do something to show respect for your parents
today.
2) Call (or write) your parents.
3) Find a way to honor your parents today.

What did you do today to observe this holiday?
Add any thoughts about your experience.

August 2
National Coloring Book Day-

The Bible passage I chose for today is
Colossians 3:15. Please, look it up and read it aloud
to the group.

Discuss how this Bible passage relates to today's
holiday.

Activity Suggestion:
1) Spend some time today coloring. It can be
relaxing, and a positive activity to distract you from
negative thoughts.

What did you do today to observe this holiday?
Add any thoughts about your experience.

August 3
National Runaway Prevention Month-

The Bible passage I chose for today is Isaiah 58:7.
Please, look it up and read it aloud to the group.

Discuss how this Bible passage relates to today's
holiday.

Activity Suggestion:
1) Discuss the many reasons why youth may run
away from home. Then, brainstorm solutions to the
problem.

What did you do today to observe this holiday?
Add any thoughts about your experience.

August 4
Admit You're Happy Day-

The Bible passage I chose for today is
1 Thessalonians 5:18. Please, look it up and read it
aloud to the group.

Discuss how this Bible passage relates to today's
holiday.

Activity Suggestions:
1) Make a list of 20 things for which you are
grateful.
2) Go through the entire day without complaining
about anything.

What did you do today to observe this holiday?
Add any thoughts about your experience.

August 5
Work Like a Dog Day-

The Bible passage I chose for today is
Proverbs 10:4-5. Please, look it up and read it aloud
to the group.

Discuss how this Bible passage relates to today's
holiday.

Activity Suggestions:
1) Show appreciation to a hard worker that you
know.
2) Do your best in whatever work you do today.
3) If you do not have employment, work at
something constructive today, and do your best.

What did you do today to observe this holiday?
Add any thoughts about your experience.

August 6
National Inventors Month-

The Bible passage I chose for today is
Genesis 4:20-22. Please, look it up and read it aloud
to the group.

Discuss how this Bible passage relates to today's
holiday.

Activity Suggestions:
1) Who is your favorite inventor or your favorite
invention? Learn more about it today.
2) If you were going to invent something, what
would it be? How would you go about doing it?

What did you do today to observe this holiday?
Add any thoughts about your experience.

August 7
Lighthouse Day-

The Bible passage I chose for today is
Psalm 119:105. Please, look it up and read it aloud
to the group.

Discuss how this Bible passage relates to today's
holiday.

Activity Suggestions:
1) Learn a little about lighthouses.
2) Visit one when you can.
3) Are you using God's word as a lighthouse? Pray
about it.

What did you do today to observe this holiday?
Add any thoughts about your experience.

August 8
Happiness Happens Day-

The Bible passage I chose for today is
1 Thessalonians 5:18. Please, look it up and read it
aloud to the group.

Discuss how this Bible passage relates to today's
holiday.

Activity Suggestion:
1) Recognize the little joys throughout the day.
Don't overlook them or take anything for granted.

What did you do today to observe this holiday?
Add any thoughts about your experience.

August 9
American Adventures Month-

The Bible passage I chose for today is
2 Corinthians 11:26. Please, look it up and read it
aloud to the group.

Discuss how this Bible passage relates to today's
holiday.

Activity Suggestion:
1) Plan an adventure for when you are able to go.
It can be local or somewhere else. Choose whatever
will be an adventure for you and those who
accompany you.

What did you do today to observe this holiday?
Add any thoughts about your experience.

August 10
National Lazy Day-

The Bible passage I chose for today is
Hebrews 4:9-10. Please, look it up and read it aloud
to the group.

Discuss how this Bible passage relates to today's
holiday.

Activity Suggestion:
1) Relax as much as you can today. Take it easy.
Rest your mind as well as your body.

What did you do today to observe this holiday?
Add any thoughts about your experience.

August 11
Bystander Awareness Month-

The Bible passage I chose for today is
Proverbs 24:10-12. Please, look it up and read it
aloud to the group.

Discuss how this Bible passage relates to today's
holiday.

Activity Suggestions:
1) Don't just stand by anymore. Do what is right.
Discuss different situations you are likely to face as
a bystander, and ways that you can respond
appropriately. It can help to be prepared for these
types of situations.
2) As an extra challenge, figure out ways for some
of these situations in which you save the victim
from the abuse without alienating the perpetrators,
but helping to change their attitudes and behavior.
This is likely not possible for severe situations, at
least not immediately. However, in cases of insult
and bullying, it could be possible.
3) As another bonus challenge, can you think of
ways to prevent any of these situations in the first
place?

What did you do today to observe this holiday?
Add any thoughts about your experience.

August 12
Middle Child Day-

The Bible passage I chose for today is
Philippians 4:11. Please, look it up and read it aloud
to the group.

Discuss how this Bible passage relates to today's
holiday.

Activity Suggestion:
1) Whether you were an only child, the oldest,
youngest, middle, etc., think about both the
advantages and disadvantages in that position. How
will this understanding help you to be kinder to
others?

What did you do today to observe this holiday?
Add any thoughts about your experience.

August 13
International Lefthander's Day-

The Bible passage I chose for today is Proverbs 4:7.
Please, look it up and read it aloud to the group.

Discuss how this Bible passage relates to today's
holiday.

Activity Suggestion:
1) Spend the day doing as much as you can (safely)
left- handed. If you are left-handed, try your right
hand today. Experiencing life from different
perspectives and challenges can be enlightening.

What did you do today to observe this holiday?
Add any thoughts about your experience.

August 14
National Immunization Awareness Month-

The Bible passage I chose for today is
Psalm 127:3. Please, look it up and read it aloud to
the group.

Discuss how this Bible passage relates to today's
holiday.

Activity Suggestion:
1) Learn all you can about immunizations, so that
you can make informed choices for yourself and
your children.

What did you do today to observe this holiday?
Add any thoughts about your experience.

August 15
Sunflower Day-

The Bible passage I chose for today is
Song of Solomon 2:12. Please, look it up and read it
aloud to the group.

Discuss how this Bible passage relates to today's
holiday.

Activity Suggestions:
1) Go for a walk or drive and look for sunflowers,
if you can..
2) Plan to plant some sunflowers next year. Make a
note. Get some seeds. Prepare an area.
3) Make a drawing or painting of a sunflower.

What did you do today to observe this holiday?
Add any thoughts about your experience.

August 16
Wave at Surveillance Day-

The Bible passage I chose for today is
Proverbs 15:13. Please, look it up and read it aloud
to the group.

Discuss how this Bible passage relates to today's
holiday.

Activity Suggestion:
1) Surveillance cameras serve an important purpose,
even if it makes some people uncomfortable at
times. This is a day to take a lighter approach and
smile and wave at the camera. It may make the
person watching it smile as well.

What did you do today to observe this holiday?
Add any thoughts about your experience.

August 17
Black Cat Appreciation Day-

The Bible passage I chose for today is
1Timothy 4:7. Please, look it up and read it aloud to
the group.

Discuss how this Bible passage relates to today's
holiday.

Activity Suggestions:
1) Put aside the superstitions and show love to
black cats.
2) Discuss other superstitions that you may
observe, and then put them aside.

What did you do today to observe this holiday?
Add any thoughts about your experience.

August 18
Serendipity (pleasant surprises) Day-

The Bible passage I chose for today is James 1:17.
Please, look it up and read it aloud to the group.

Discuss how this Bible passage relates to today's
holiday.

Activity Suggestion:
1) Notice those pleasant little surprises throughout
the day, and remember to thank God for them.

What did you do today to observe this holiday?
Add any thoughts about your experience.

August 19
World Humanitarian Day-

The Bible passage I chose for today is John 15:13.
Please, look it up and read it aloud to the group.

Discuss how this Bible passage relates to today's
holiday.

Activity Suggestions:
1) This is a day to appreciate those putting
themselves in danger to help those in need. Find a
way to show appreciation to them.
2) Send a thank you card to police, firefighters,
EMT's, etc.

What did you do today to observe this holiday?
Add any thoughts about your experience.

August 20
National Radio Day-

The Bible passage I chose for today is
Philippians 4:8. Please, look it up and read it aloud
to the group.

Discuss how this Bible passage relates to today's
holiday.

Activity Suggestion:
1) Spend some time today listening to a Christian
radio station.

What did you do today to observe this holiday?
Add any thoughts about your experience.

August 21
Senior Citizens Day-

The Bible passage I chose for today is
Leviticus 19:32. Please, look it up and read it aloud
to the group.

Discuss how this Bible passage relates to today's
holiday.

Activity Suggestions:
1) Learn about, and celebrate, the wisdom and
achievements senior citizens have made.
2) Advocate for the rights of older people
throughout the world when and how you can.

What did you do today to observe this holiday?
Add any thoughts about your experience.

August 22
What Will Be Your Legacy Month-

The Bible passage I chose for today is
Psalm 103:17. Please, look it up and read it aloud to
the group.

Discuss how this Bible passage relates to today's
holiday.

Activity Suggestion:
1) Think about how you want to be remembered,
and what you want to teach your children (if you
have or are going to have them) while you are still
alive.

What did you do today to observe this holiday?
Add any thoughts about your experience.

August 23
Day for the Remembrance of the Slave Trade & Its Abolition-

The Bible passage I chose for today is
Exodus 21:16. Please, look it up and read it aloud
to the group.
*Note: Remember that punishment for sins is not up to you.
This verse is used to show that this is a sin, and what the
punishment was at that time and place.*

Discuss how this Bible passage relates to today's
holiday.

Activity Suggestions:
1) Sadly, there are still many forms of slavery today.
Learn about and support organizations that work to
end human trafficking.
2) Share information about this problem and these
organizations on social media.

What did you do today to observe this holiday?
Add any thoughts about your experience.

August 24
National Win with Civility Month-

The Bible passage I chose for today is
Romans 12:18. Please, look it up and read it aloud
to the group.

Discuss how this Bible passage relates to today's
holiday.

Activity Suggestion:
1) Is there someone who gets on your nerves?
Instead of thinking of witty and cutting replies,
spend some time thinking about how to answer
that person (or those types of comments in general)
in a way that diffuses the situation, and possibly
changes the person's attitude/behavior, while being
respectful. Believe me, this can take a lot more
thought than "witty" comments.

What did you do today to observe this holiday?
Add any thoughts about your experience.

August 25
National Eye Exam Month-

The Bible passage I chose for today is
Deuteronomy 34:7. Please, look it up and read it
aloud to the group.

Discuss how this Bible passage relates to today's
holiday.

Activity Suggestion:
1) Make sure you and your family are up-to-date on
your eye exams. Request an eye appointment if you
have not had one recently, and especially if you
have any issues with your eyes.

What did you do today to observe this holiday?
Add any thoughts about your experience.

August 26
Women's Equality Day-

The Bible passage I chose for today is
Galatians 3:28. Please, look it up and read it aloud
to the group.

Discuss how this Bible passage relates to today's
holiday.

Activity Suggestions:
1) Be conscious to refrain from any sexist talk, no
matter what gender you are. Treat everyone with
respect.
2) Do not tell or laugh at sexist jokes, watch sexist
shows, or listen to sexist music.

What did you do today to observe this holiday?
Add any thoughts about your experience.

August 27
Just Because Day-

The Bible passage I chose for today is
Romans 12:10. Please, look it up and read it aloud
to the group.

Discuss how this Bible passage relates to today's
holiday.

Activity Suggestion:
1) Make (or buy) someone a card, not because it is
their birthday or other holiday, but just because
you're thinking of them.

What did you do today to observe this holiday?
Add any thoughts about your experience.

August 28
Happily Married Husband and Wife Week-
Spend some special time with your spouse today.

The Bible passage I chose for today is 1 Peter 3:1-7.
Please, look it up and read it aloud to the group.

Discuss how this Bible passage relates to today's
holiday.

Activity Suggestions:
1) Spend some special time with your spouse today.
2) If you cannot spend time with your spouse, call
or write them.
3) If you are not married, be sure you are respecting
the relationships of others. Do not flirt with a
married person (or anyone in an exclusive
relationship), and do not encourage them to be
disrespectful to their spouse (or partner) in any way,
even in joking.

What did you do today to observe this holiday?
Add any thoughts about your experience.

August 29
Individual Rights Day-

The Bible passage I chose for today is
Romans 13:1-10. Please, look it up and read it aloud
to the group.

Discuss how this Bible passage relates to today's
holiday.

Activity Suggestion:
1) Read to learn what your constitutional rights
really are. Look up the actual constitution,
especially the amendments, rather than someone
else's explanation of it.

What did you do today to observe this holiday?
Add any thoughts about your experience.

August 30
National Grief Awareness Day-

The Bible passage I chose for today is
Revelation 21:4. Please, look it up and read it aloud
to the group.

Discuss how this Bible passage relates to today's
holiday.

Activity Suggestions:
1) Spend time with someone who is grieving. Listen
and let them know you care.
2) If you cannot be there in person, call or write
them and keep in touch.

What did you do today to observe this holiday?
Add any thoughts about your experience.

August 31
Eat Outside Day-

The Bible passage I chose for today is
Romans 15:7. Please, look it up and read it aloud to
the group.

Discuss how this Bible passage relates to today's
holiday.

Activity Suggestion:
1) If you can, have your lunch outside today. Invite
others to join you. Specifically invite someone who
is not normally included in your group, and may
appreciate the invitation.

What did you do today to observe this holiday?
Add any thoughts about your experience.

10

SEPTEMBER

September 1
Random Acts of Kindness Day (New Zealand)-

The Bible passage I chose for today is
Ephesians 4:32. Please, look it up and read it aloud
to the group.

Discuss how this Bible passage relates to today's
holiday.

Activity Suggestion:
1) Commit an act of kindness. You can plan it or
just seize an opportunity sometime during your day.

What did you do today to observe this holiday?
Add any thoughts about your experience.

September 2
International Enthusiasm Week-

The Bible passage I chose for today is
Colossians 3:23. Please, look it up and read it aloud
to the group.

Discuss how this Bible passage relates to today's
holiday.

Activity Suggestions:
1) Spend some time doing something you are
enthusiastic about this week.
2) If it's been so long you don't feel enthusiastic
about anything, take some time to think about what
you used to get excited about.

What did you do today to observe this holiday?
Add any thoughts about your experience.

September 3
Children's Good Manners Month-

The Bible passage I chose for today is
Deuteronomy 6:6-7. Please, look it up and read it
aloud to the group.

Discuss how this Bible passage relates to today's
holiday.

Activity Suggestions:
1) Spend some time today
learning/teaching/reinforcing good manners.
2) Make sure that you are a good example of the
manners you are trying to teach. Everyone is a role
model to others, so be the best one you can be.

What did you do today to observe this holiday?
Add any thoughts about your experience.

September 4
International Self-Awareness Month-

The Bible passage I chose for today is
Romans 12:3-8. Please, look it up and read it aloud
to the group.

Discuss how this Bible passage relates to today's
holiday.

Activity Suggestions:
1) Spend some time throughout your day thinking
about why you think or do things the way you do.
2) Spend some time today thinking about the gifts
that you have, and how you can best put them to
use.

What did you do today to observe this holiday?
Add any thoughts about your experience.

September 5
International Day of Charity-

The Bible passage I chose for today is
2 Corinthians 9:7. Please, look it up and read it
aloud to the group.

Discuss how this Bible passage relates to today's
holiday.

Activity Suggestion:
1) Today, find a way to give of yourself to help
someone else.

What did you do today to observe this holiday?
Add any thoughts about your experience.

September 6
International Speak Out Month-

The Bible passage I chose for today is James 4:17.
Please, look it up and read it aloud to the group.

Discuss how this Bible passage relates to today's
holiday.

Activity Suggestion:
1) This is a day to think about what causes you
believe in, and speak out for them. Make sure you
are respectful in stating your opinions and
supporting your cause.

What did you do today to observe this holiday?
Add any thoughts about your experience.

September 7
Grandma Moses Day-

The Bible passage I chose for today is
Leviticus 19:32. Please, look it up and read it aloud
to the group.

Discuss how this Bible passage relates to today's
holiday.

Activity Suggestion:
1) Spend some time today learning about Grandma
Moses and looking at some of her paintings.

What did you do today to observe this holiday?
Add any thoughts about your experience.

September 8
Pardon Day-

The Bible passage I chose for today is
Ephesians 4:31. Please, look it up and read it aloud
to the group.

Discuss how this Bible passage relates to today's
holiday.

Activity Suggestion:
1) Even if you aren't the president, who can you
pardon today? Are you holding any grudges? Have
you been punishing someone (consciously or
unconsciously) for something they have done in the
past? Become aware of it and pardon them. Wipe
the slate clean.

What did you do today to observe this holiday?
Add any thoughts about your experience.

September 9
National Prosper Where You Are Planted
Month-

The Bible passage I chose for today is Isaiah 43:2.
Please, look it up and read it aloud to the group.

Discuss how this Bible passage relates to today's
holiday.

Activity Suggestion:
1) Sometimes we find ourselves in places or
situations we don't enjoy. Maybe we are forced to
move or change schools or jobs. Maybe we really
want to and can't. This is an opportunity to remind
us to make the best of WHAT IS. What can you do
to make life better right where you are?

What did you do today to observe this holiday?
Add any thoughts about your experience.

September 10
(World) Suicide Prevention Day-

The Bible passage I chose for today is
Ecclesiastes 4:9-12. Please, look it up and read it
aloud to the group.

Discuss how this Bible passage relates to today's
holiday.

Activity Suggestions:
1) Learn to recognize the signs of depression and
those of people contemplating suicide.
2) Share the information on social media.
3) Do you know anyone who is struggling? Take up
some extra time with that person. Let him/her
know you are there and you care.
4) If you are struggling, seek help.

What did you do today to observe this holiday?
Add any thoughts about your experience.

September 11
National Day of Service and Remembrance-

The Bible passage I chose for today is 1 Peter 4:10. Please, look it up and read it aloud to the group.

Discuss how this Bible passage relates to today's holiday.

Activity Suggestion:
1) Engage in some type of community service in honor of those who risked/lost their lives helping others on 9/11. Be creative. Do what you can where you are.

What did you do today to observe this holiday? Add any thoughts about your experience.

September 12
National Infant Mortality Awareness Month-

The Bible passage I chose for today is Psalm 82:3.
Please, look it up and read it aloud to the group.

Discuss how this Bible passage relates to today's
holiday.

Activity Suggestion:
1) Become informed about, and spread awareness
of, infant mortality causes and prevention to keep
infants safe.

What did you do today to observe this holiday?
Add any thoughts about your experience.

September 13
Defy Superstitions Day-

The Bible passage I chose for today is
1 Timothy 4:7. Please, look it up and read it aloud
to the group.

Discuss how this Bible passage relates to today's
holiday.

Activity Suggestion:
1) Recognize superstitions for what they are. They
are attributing power to ridiculous things. Trust in
God instead of superstitions.

What did you do today to observe this holiday?
Add any thoughts about your experience.

September 14
National Quiet Day-

The Bible passage I chose for today is
Proverbs 10:19. Please, look it up and read it aloud
to the group.

Discuss how this Bible passage relates to today's
holiday.

Activity Suggestion:
1) Enjoy some peace and quiet today. Don't try to
fill every silence with conversation, music, tv, etc.
Take some time to enjoy the silence.

What did you do today to observe this holiday?
Add any thoughts about your experience.

September 15
Self Improvement Month-

The Bible passage I chose for today is
Ephesians 4:20-24. Please, look it up and read it
aloud to the group.

Discuss how this Bible passage relates to today's
holiday.

Activity Suggestion:
1) Choose one thing you'd like to improve upon,
then plan and implement steps towards that
improvement.

What did you do today to observe this holiday?
Add any thoughts about your experience.

September 16
Play Dough Day-

The Bible passage I chose for today is
Psalm 90:17. Please, look it up and read it aloud to
the group.

Discuss how this Bible passage relates to today's
holiday.

Activity Suggestion:
1) Make some homemade play dough. Then, enjoy
creating. You may choose to dry and then paint
your creations. Just be sure that you do not eat or
drink out of your creations, such as if you made a
bowl or cup, because this wouldn't be the right kind
of clay and your paint is probably not well suited
for that, either.

What did you do today to observe this holiday?
Add any thoughts about your experience.

September 17
Citizenship Day-

The Bible passage I chose for today is
Leviticus 19:33-34. Please, look it up and read it
aloud to the group.

Discuss how this Bible passage relates to today's
holiday.

Activity Suggestion:
1) Look up and take a practice citizenship test so
that you learn what it takes to become a citizen, and
if you have that knowledge. Natural born citizens
should have the knowledge expected of those who
wish to become citizens.

What did you do today to observe this holiday?
Add any thoughts about your experience.

September 18
National Respect Day-

The Bible passage I chose for today is
Proverbs 16:32. Please, look it up and read it aloud
to the group.

Discuss how this Bible passage relates to today's
holiday.

Activity Suggestions:
1) Make a real effort to be respectful of everyone,
regardless of how you feel about them, what they
say, or how they act. It doesn't mean you don't set
boundaries or that you go along with them, but be
respectful.
2) Discuss as a group ways of disagreeing with
someone while staying respectful.

What did you do today to observe this holiday?
Add any thoughts about your experience.

September 19
National Recovery Month-

The Bible passage I chose for today is
1 Corinthians 10:13. Please, look it up and read it
aloud to the group.

Discuss how this Bible passage relates to today's
holiday.

Activity Suggestions:
1) If you have any addictions, get the help you need
to work towards recovery.
2) If you know someone who is in recovery, find a
way to provide some support.

What did you do today to observe this holiday?
Add any thoughts about your experience.

September 20
National Preparedness Month-

The Bible passage I chose for today is
Proverbs 6:6-8. Please, look it up and read it aloud
to the group.

Discuss how this Bible passage relates to today's
holiday.

Activity Suggestions:
1) Learn how to be prepared for disasters.
2) You may want to consider taking first aid and
CPR training, and learn the Heimlich Maneuver.

What did you do today to observe this holiday?
Add any thoughts about your experience.

September 21
International Day of Peace -

The Bible passage I chose for today is
Romans 12:18. Please, look it up and read it aloud
to the group.

Discuss how this Bible passage relates to today's
holiday.

Activity Suggestion:
1) Do you need to make peace with anyone, or talk
over anything that could be difficult? Prepare
yourself, and have the conversation.

What did you do today to observe this holiday?
Add any thoughts about your experience.

September 22
Dear Diary Day-

The Bible passage I chose for today is
2 Corinthians 10:3-5. Please, look it up and read it
aloud to the group.

Discuss how this Bible passage relates to today's
holiday.

Activity Suggestion:
1) Spend some time today journaling. It can help
you process your thoughts in a positive way. (If you
are upset, it can help to slow down your writing.
That can help calm down your system and help you
feel calmer.)

What did you do today to observe this holiday?
Add any thoughts about your experience.

September 23
Healthy Aging Month-

The Bible passage I chose for today is
Proverbs 16:31. Please, look it up and read it aloud
to the group.

Discuss how this Bible passage relates to today's
holiday.

Activity Suggestions:
1) You can surely work at staying young and
healthy, but don't let it get you to try desperation
tactics to fight the aging process, or let the changes
of aging get you down.
2) Find out the recommended amount of water you
should be drinking, and try to drink that much each
day.

What did you do today to observe this holiday?
Add any thoughts about your experience.

September 24
Gallbladder Good Health Day-

The Bible passage I chose for today is
Proverbs 18:15. Please, look it up and read it aloud
to the group.

Discuss how this Bible passage relates to today's
holiday.

Activity Suggestion:
1) Learn about the gallbladder, and the best way to
take care of it.

What did you do today to observe this holiday?
Add any thoughts about your experience.

September 25
World Dream Day-

The Bible passage I chose for today is
1 Peter 3:10-12. Please, look it up and read it aloud
to the group.

Discuss how this Bible passage relates to today's
holiday.

Activity Suggestion:
1) What is a dream that you have for the world?
What is one step you can take to make it come
true?

What did you do today to observe this holiday?
Add any thoughts about your experience.

September 26
Situational Awareness Day-

The Bible passage I chose for today is
Matthew 24:24. Please, look it up and read it aloud
to the group.

Discuss how this Bible passage relates to today's
holiday.

Activity Suggestion:
1) Look up tips to improve situational awareness.
How much do you pay attention to what is going
on around you? Try to improve on that, if there is
room for improvement.

What did you do today to observe this holiday?
Add any thoughts about your experience.

September 27
Superior Relationships Month-

The Bible passage I chose for today is
Colossians 3:16-21. Please, look it up and read it
aloud to the group.

Discuss how this Bible passage relates to today's
holiday.

Activity Suggestions:
1) Read what the Bible has to say about the roles of
husbands and wives, and grow your relationship the
way God wants. Hint: It's not one-sided or just a
couple of verses, although I'm only including one
passage here.
2) Use this passage to help guide all your
relationships with others.

What did you do today to observe this holiday?
Add any thoughts about your experience.

September 28
International People Skills Month-

The Bible passage I chose for today is
Proverbs 15:1-2. Please, look it up and read it aloud
to the group.

Discuss how this Bible passage relates to today's
holiday.

Activity Suggestion:
1) Think of ways to improve your people skills.
Look everyone in the eye. Smile. Talk with people,
not at them. Be respectful when you disagree. What
else can you do?

What did you do today to observe this holiday?
Add any thoughts about your experience.

September 29
Broadway Musicals Day-

The Bible passage I chose for today is
Ecclesiastes 3:1-8. Please, look it up and read it
aloud to the group.

Discuss how this Bible passage relates to today's
holiday.

Activity Suggestion:
1) As a group, choose and watch a Broadway
musical on television or online.

What did you do today to observe this holiday?
Add any thoughts about your experience.

September 30
Pain Awareness Month-

The Bible passage I chose for today is
Colossians 4:6. Please, look it up and read it aloud
to the group.

Discuss how this Bible passage relates to today's
holiday.

Activity Suggestion:
1) Learn about conditions that cause chronic pain.
It can be very helpful to have an understanding of
other people's experiences.

What did you do today to observe this holiday?
Add any thoughts about your experience.

October 1
International Day of Older
Persons/International Music Day-

The Bible passage I chose for today is
Leviticus 19:32. Please, look it up and read it aloud
to the group.

Discuss how this Bible passage relates to today's
holiday.

Activity Suggestions:
1) Try to arrange a visit with an elderly person in
your life.
2) If you cannot visit, call or write an elderly person
in your life.
3) Listen to music (make sure it's appropriate) from
an older generation. The farther back in time you
go, the less likely it is that any of the music will
have inappropriate language.

What did you do today to observe this holiday?
Add any thoughts about your experience.

October 2
National Custodial Workers Day-

The Bible passage I chose for today is
Ephesians 6:7. Please, look it up and read it aloud
to the group.

Discuss how this Bible passage relates to today's
holiday.

Activity Suggestions:
1) Thank the custodial workers in your life.
2) You may even want to give them a token of
appreciation and/or find a way to do something for
them.

What did you do today to observe this holiday?
Add any thoughts about your experience.

October 3
Bullying Prevention Month-

The Bible passage I chose for today is Psalm 1:1-2.
Please, look it up and read it aloud to the group.

Discuss how this Bible passage relates to today's
holiday.

Activity Suggestions:
What can YOU do to end bullying?
1) You can model respectful behavior to
EVERYONE.
2) You can stand up for those who are bullied.
3) You can be careful what you laugh at.
4) You can discourage disrespectful talk before it
turns into actions.

What did you do today to observe this holiday?
Add any thoughts about your experience.

October 4
World Animal Day-

The Bible passage I chose for today is Genesis 1:30. Please, look it up and read it aloud to the group.

Discuss how this Bible passage relates to today's holiday.

Activity Suggestions:
1) Watch an animal show with the group. This could be a documentary, a performance, or anything that you choose that is respectful to the animals.
2) Make a painting or drawing with animals of your choice. As always, you could choose to keep your art or bless someone else with it.

What did you do today to observe this holiday? Add any thoughts about your experience.

October 5
World Teachers Day-

The Bible passage I chose for today is Luke 6:40.
Please, look it up and read it aloud to the group.

Discuss how this Bible passage relates to today's
holiday.

Activity Suggestions:
*This is a day to show appreciation to the teachers in your life
and everywhere.*
1) Thank a teacher.
2) Send a card to a teacher you once had that made
a difference in your life.
3) Send a card to a teacher your children once had
that made a difference in their lives.

What did you do today to observe this holiday?
Add any thoughts about your experience.

October 6
American Libraries Day-

The Bible passage I chose for today is
Proverbs 18:15. Please, look it up and read it aloud
to the group.

Discuss how this Bible passage relates to today's
holiday.

Activity Suggestions:
1) Do you have a current library card? If not, get
one, and check out a book or movie.
2) If you are currently staying in a facility, and they
have a library, check out a book from there to read.

What did you do today to observe this holiday?
Add any thoughts about your experience.

October 7
You Matter to Me Day-

The Bible passage I chose for today is Luke 15:1-7.
Please, look it up and read it aloud to the group.

Discuss how this Bible passage relates to today's
holiday.

Activity Suggestion:
1) Think of someone in your life that may feel
taken for granted. Find a way to show that person
that he/she matters.

What did you do today to observe this holiday?
Add any thoughts about your experience.

October 8
Domestic Violence Awareness Month-

The Bible passage I chose for today is
Psalm 82:2-4. Please, look it up and read it aloud to
the group.

Discuss how this Bible passage relates to today's
holiday.

Activity Suggestions:
1) Learn about, and then find a way to raise
awareness of, domestic violence.
2) If you know anyone in danger, find a way to be
supportive and assist him/her in getting help.

What did you do today to observe this holiday?
Add any thoughts about your experience.

October 9
Eat Better, Eat Together Month-

The Bible passage I chose for today is Acts 2:46.
Please, look it up and read it aloud to the group.

Discuss how this Bible passage relates to today's
holiday.

Activity Suggestion:
1) Make healthy food choices, and try to be sociable
at mealtime. Have pleasant discussions with others.
Invite those who sit alone to sit with you.

What did you do today to observe this holiday?
Add any thoughts about your experience.

October 10
World Mental Health Day-

The Bible passage I chose for today is
1 Kings 19:1-18. Please, look it up and read it aloud
to the group.

Discuss how this Bible passage relates to today's
holiday.

Activity Suggestions:
1) If you know someone with a mental health issue,
learn a little about it. If you don't, choose a mental
health condition to learn about.
2) If you know someone with a mental health issue,
find a way to be supportive.
3) If you have a mental health issue, get the help
that you need, and do what you need to do to stay
healthy.

What did you do today to observe this holiday?
Add any thoughts about your experience.

October 11
World Obesity Day-

The Bible passage I chose for today is
3 John 1:2. Please, look it up and read it aloud to
the group.

Discuss how this Bible passage relates to today's
holiday.

Activity Suggestions:
1) Learn about the physical and mental health
effects of obesity.
2) Do not make fun of anyone's body size or shape.
3) Find out how much water you should be
drinking each day, and try to meet that requirement.
4) Make healthy food choices.
5) Try to exercise a little each day.

What did you do today to observe this holiday?
Add any thoughts about your experience.

October 12
National Cyber Security Awareness Month-

The Bible passage I chose for today is Psalm 46:1.
Please, look it up and read it aloud to the group.

Discuss how this Bible passage relates to today's
holiday.

Activity Suggestion:
1) Educate yourself on how to keep you and your
family safe online.

What did you do today to observe this holiday?
Add any thoughts about your experience.

October 13
Good Samaritan Day-

The Bible passage I chose for today is
Luke 10:25-37. Please, look it up and read it aloud
to the group.

Discuss how this Bible passage relates to today's
holiday.

Activity Suggestion:
1) Choose something you can do today to be a
good neighbor to someone.

What did you do today to observe this holiday?
Add any thoughts about your experience.

October 14
National Stop Bullying Day-

The Bible passage I chose for today is
Hebrews 13:1-2. Please, look it up and read it aloud
to the group.

Discuss how this Bible passage relates to today's
holiday.

Activity Suggestions:
1) Let's use this day to focus on treating people
with respect and kindness.
2) Don't just think about the neighbor you can see,
but the neighbors you may never meet as well.

What did you do today to observe this holiday?
Add any thoughts about your experience.

October 15
National Grouch Day-

The Bible passage I chose for today is
Romans 15:2. Please, look it up and read it aloud to
the group.

Discuss how this Bible passage relates to today's
holiday.

Activity Suggestion:
1) Choose the grouchiest person you know, and do
something to make their day happier. (Do not hurt
their feelings by letting them know you think they
are grouchy.)

What did you do today to observe this holiday?
Add any thoughts about your experience.

October 16
National Dictionary Day-

The Bible passage I chose for today is
Proverbs 18:15. Please, look it up and read it aloud
to the group.

Discuss how this Bible passage relates to today's
holiday.

Activity Suggestion:
1) Pass around a dictionary, and have each person
randomly select a word to learn and write down.
When each person has learned a new word, let each
person share them with the group.

What did you do today to observe this holiday?
Add any thoughts about your experience.

October 17
Talk About Medicines Month/ National Substance Abuse Prevention Month-

The Bible passage I chose for today is
1 Corinthians 10:13. Please, look it up and read it aloud to the group.

Discuss how this Bible passage relates to today's holiday.

Activity Suggestions:
1) Learn about medications that can be addictive.
2) Only take what you need, when you need it, and as prescribed.
3) Properly dispose of unused medications through community drop-offs.
4) Keep medications locked up so that other people are not tempted to take them.
5) Seek professional help if you find yourself craving or abusing any medications, drugs, or alcohol.

What did you do today to observe this holiday?
Add any thoughts about your experience.

October 18
National Sarcastic Awareness Month-

The Bible passage I chose for today is 1 Peter 3:8.
Please, look it up and read it aloud to the group.

Discuss how this Bible passage relates to today's
holiday.

Activity Suggestion:
1) As Christians, we are not going to glorify
sarcasm. Rather, we will be aware of when we use it
and try to eliminate it from our lives.

What did you do today to observe this holiday?
Add any thoughts about your experience.

October 19
Evaluate Your Life Day-

The Bible passage I chose for today is Psalm 5:8.
Please, look it up and read it aloud to the group.

Discuss how this Bible passage relates to today's
holiday.

Activity Suggestion:
1) This is a great day to think about your life, if it is
going the way you would like, and what changes
you would like to make.

What did you do today to observe this holiday?
Add any thoughts about your experience.

October 20
National Osteoporosis Day-

The Bible passage I chose for today is 3 John 1:2.
Please, look it up and read it aloud to the group.

Discuss how this Bible passage relates to today's
holiday.

Activity Suggestion:
1) Learn what you can do to maintain, and even
improve, your bone health.

What did you do today to observe this holiday?
Add any thoughts about your experience.

October 21
Celebration of the Mind Day-

The Bible passage I chose for today is
Proverbs 3:13. Please, look it up and read it aloud
to the group.

Discuss how this Bible passage relates to today's
holiday.

Activity Suggestion:
1) This is a day for puzzles, math, critical thinking,
and any intellectual challenge. Engage in any of
these activities that you choose.

What did you do today to observe this holiday?
Add any thoughts about your experience.

October 22
Smart is Cool Day-

The Bible passage I chose for today is Luke 2:52.
Please, look it up and read it aloud to the group.

Discuss how this Bible passage relates to today's
holiday.

Activity Suggestions:
1) Don't make fun of intelligence, call anybody a
nerd or geek, or act less intelligent to fit in with
others.
2) Be yourself, and respect the gifts of others
without being defensive or mocking them.

What did you do today to observe this holiday?
Add any thoughts about your experience.

October 23
National Sudden Infant Death Syndrome
Awareness Month-

The Bible passage I chose for today is
Psalm 127:3. Please, look it up and read it aloud to
the group.

Discuss how this Bible passage relates to today's
holiday.

Activity Suggestion:
1) Learn about SIDS and how to prevent it.

What did you do today to observe this holiday?
Add any thoughts about your experience.

October 24
Organize Your Medical Information Month-

The Bible passage I chose for today is
Proverbs 23:19. Please, look it up and read it aloud
to the group.

Discuss how this Bible passage relates to today's
holiday.

Activity Suggestion:
1) Start or update a medical file or folder for each
member of your family.

What did you do today to observe this holiday?
Add any thoughts about your experience.

October 25
Positive Attitude Month-

The Bible passage I chose for today is
Philippians 4:8-9. Please, look it up and read it
aloud to the group.

Discuss how this Bible passage relates to today's
holiday.

Activity Suggestion:
1) Spend the day being aware of your thoughts,
keeping them in line with today's Bible verse.

What did you do today to observe this holiday?
Add any thoughts about your experience.

October 26
Day of the Deployed-

The Bible passage I chose for today is
Psalm 144:1-2. Please, look it up and read it aloud
to the group.

Discuss how this Bible passage relates to today's
holiday.

Activity Suggestions:
1) Pray for those who are deployed in the military.
2) If you know a family who has a member who is
deployed, find a way to be a comfort and a blessing
to them.

What did you do today to observe this holiday?
Add any thoughts about your experience.

October 27
Cranky Coworkers Day-

The Bible passage I chose for today is
Luke 6:27-28. Please, look it up and read it aloud to
the group.

Discuss how this Bible passage relates to today's
holiday.

Activity Suggestions:
1) The challenge today is to help that co-worker
have a better outlook on life. Smile, be kind, and
include this person in conversations at break.
2) If you are not employed, choose someone else
that you know, and brighten their day.

What did you do today to observe this holiday?
Add any thoughts about your experience.

October 28
National First Responders Day-

The Bible passage I chose for today is John 15:13.
Please, look it up and read it aloud to the group.

Discuss how this Bible passage relates to today's
holiday.

Activity Suggestions:
1) Learn about the different types of first
responders that we have.
2) Find a way to show appreciation to these brave
and kind workers today.

What did you do today to observe this holiday?
Add any thoughts about your experience.

October 29
World Stroke Day-

The Bible passage I chose for today is James 1:2-7.
Please, look it up and read it aloud to the group.

Discuss how this Bible passage relates to today's
holiday.

Activity Suggestion:
1) Learn what you can about stroke prevention, and
implement any lifestyle changes that would be
helpful.

What did you do today to observe this holiday?
Add any thoughts about your experience.

October 30
Emotional Intelligence Awareness
Month/Emotional Wellness Month-

The Bible passage I chose for today is Romans 8:6.
Please, look it up and read it aloud to the group.

Discuss how this Bible passage relates to today's
holiday.

Activity Suggestion:
1) This is a good day to think about what you need
for emotional wellness. Do you need more positive
social interactions? Time to relax built into your
day? More sleep at night? To take the time for
proper nutrition rather than eating out of the
vending machines? More time for prayer and
reading the Bible?

What did you do today to observe this holiday?
Add any thoughts about your experience.

October 31
National Knock Knock Jokes Day-

The Bible passage I chose for today is
Proverbs 17:22. Please, look it up and read it aloud
to the group.

Discuss how this Bible passage relates to today's
holiday.

Activity Suggestion:
1) Have fun telling (appropriate) knock knock jokes
with your group, and with others throughout the
day.

What did you do today to observe this holiday?
Add any thoughts about your experience.

November 1
Extra Mile Day/ National Family Caregiver Day-

The Bible passage I chose for today is Galatians 6:2. Please, look it up and read it aloud to the group.

Discuss how this Bible passage relates to today's holiday.

Activity Suggestion:
1) Go out of your way to do something nice for someone who devotes themselves to others.

What did you do today to observe this holiday? Add any thoughts about your experience.

November 2
Plan Your Epitaph Day-

The Bible passage I chose for today is Acts 11:24.
Please, look it up and read it aloud to the group.

Discuss how this Bible passage relates to today's
holiday.

Activity Suggestion:
1) How do you want to be remembered? What do
you need to change for that to be a reality?

What did you do today to observe this holiday?
Add any thoughts about your experience.

November 3
Public Television Day-

The Bible passage I chose for today is
Proverbs 18:15. Please, look it up and read it aloud
to the group.

Discuss how this Bible passage relates to today's
holiday.

Activity Suggestion:
1) Find some shows on public television that you
want to watch today.

What did you do today to observe this holiday?
Add any thoughts about your experience.

November 4
Use Your Common Sense Day-

The Bible passage I chose for today is Proverbs 2:6.
Please, look it up and read it aloud to the group.

Discuss how this Bible passage relates to today's
holiday.

Activity Suggestions:
1) When you are struggling with a decision, pray
about it. Ask God for wisdom.
2) Do what you know is right, instead of following
the crowd or an impulse you may have.

What did you do today to observe this holiday?
Add any thoughts about your experience.

November 5
American Football Day-

The Bible passage I chose for today is
2 Timothy 2:5. Please, look it up and read it aloud
to the group.

Discuss how this Bible passage relates to today's
holiday.

Activity Suggestions:
1) Play a game of football together as a group.
2) Watch football on television together. Even if
you have a favorite team, be impartial in how you
judge behaviors and calls, and pray for all on both
teams to be safe from injury, and for healing if they
are injured.

What did you do today to observe this holiday?
Add any thoughts about your experience.

November 6
Saxophone Day-

The Bible passage I chose for today is Psalm 98:4.
Please, look it up and read it aloud to the group.

Discuss how this Bible passage relates to today's
holiday.

Activity Suggestions:
1) Listen to some jazz music together as a group.
See if you can find some Christian jazz to play.

What did you do today to observe this holiday?
Add any thoughts about your experience.

November 7
America Recycles Month-

The Bible passage I chose for today is Genesis 2:15.
Please, look it up and read it aloud to the group.

Discuss how this Bible passage relates to today's
holiday.

Activity Suggestion:
1) Learn what your city accepts in its recycling, and
do what you can to recycle everything that can be
recycled.

What did you do today to observe this holiday?
Add any thoughts about your experience.

November 8
National Parents as Teachers Day-

The Bible passage I chose for today is
Proverbs 22:6. Please, look it up and read it aloud
to the group.

Discuss how this Bible passage relates to today's
holiday.

Activity Suggestions:
1) Parents are their children's first and most
important teachers. This is a day for parents to be
conscious of being a good example to their
children, and the parents of small children to make
the effort to help their children to become ready for
school.
2) We can all help to support parents, or programs
that help parents, in these efforts. What can you do
today?
3) Ask your parents their opinions about
something, and truly listen.

What did you do today to observe this holiday?
Add any thoughts about your experience.

November 9
Admitting Your Mistakes Day-

The Bible passage I chose for today is
Psalm 51:2-3. Please, look it up and read it aloud to
the group.

Discuss how this Bible passage relates to today's
holiday.

Activity Suggestions:
1) Admit when you make a mistake. Do not try to
blame someone or something else. Do what you
can to make up for the mistake, if there were any
consequences to anyone.
2) If it was a sin, also pray to God for forgiveness,
and then repent (turn from that sin, trying not to do
that anymore). And then, let it go. It doesn't help
anyone to dwell on past mistakes. If you've
admitted it, made amends the best you can, prayed
and repented, you've done what you can. I believe
you will be much more useful to God and others if
you are not living in a pit of condemnation. God
forgives. Satan tries to convince us we are
permanently condemned.

What did you do today to observe this holiday?
Add any thoughts about your experience.

November 10
Lung Cancer Awareness Month-

The Bible passage I chose for today is
1 Corinthians 6:19-20. Please, look it up and read it
aloud to the group.

Discuss how this Bible passage relates to today's
holiday.

Activity Suggestions:
1) Please, quit smoking. Get the help that you need.
There are programs that offer free support and
nicotine replacement.
2) Don't harass others to quit, but be as supportive
as you can be to help them.
3) Avoid second-hand smoke as much as you can.
Learn about other threats to your lungs, and how
best to stay safe and healthy.

What did you do today to observe this holiday?
Add any thoughts about your experience.

November 11
Veteran's Day-

The Bible passage I chose for today is Galatians 5:1.
Please, look it up and read it aloud to the group.

Discuss how this Bible passage relates to today's
holiday.

Activity Suggestions:
1) This is a day to honor and thank all those who
have served in the military, fighting for our
freedoms here on Earth, including our religious
freedoms.
2) If you cannot thank a veteran in person, call,
write, send a thank you note, or whatever you can
do.

What did you do today to observe this holiday?
Add any thoughts about your experience.

November 12
Military Family Appreciation Month-

The Bible passage I chose for today is Galatians 5:1.
Please, look it up and read it aloud to the group.

Discuss how this Bible passage relates to today's
holiday.

Activity Suggestions:
*The family makes sacrifices, too, and it is so that we can all
have our freedoms here on Earth, including religious freedom.*
1) If you know a military family, thank them for
their service.
2) Make a post on social media thanking military
families for their sacrifices.
3) Join an organization that sends cards, letters, or
packages to military members and their families.

What did you do today to observe this holiday?
Add any thoughts about your experience.

November 13
World Kindness Day-

The Bible passage I chose for today is
Philippians 2:3. Please, look it up and read it aloud
to the group.

Discuss how this Bible passage relates to today's
holiday.

Activity Suggestions:
1) Let someone go first in line or in traffic.
2) Open the door for others.
3) Choose your own act of kindness.

What did you do today to observe this holiday?
Add any thoughts about your experience.

November 14
Loosen Up, Lighten Up Day-

The Bible passage I chose for today is
Romans 14:13. Please, look it up and read it aloud
to the group.

Discuss how this Bible passage relates to today's
holiday.

Activity Suggestion:
1) Think of the things that you are rigid about,
something that you think has to be done one
specific way (and yet others successfully do it
another), such as folding towels or loading a
dishwasher. If someone else is doing the task, let it
go. Thank the person for doing the task.

What did you do today to observe this holiday?
Add any thoughts about your experience.

November 15
I Love to Write Day-

The Bible passage I chose for today is
1 Timothy 3:14. Please, look it up and read it aloud
to the group.

Discuss how this Bible passage relates to today's
holiday.

Activity Suggestions:
1) Write a story.
2) Write your autobiography.
3) Write a letter.
4) Write in your journal. Start a journal if you don't
already have one.

What did you do today to observe this holiday?
Add any thoughts about your experience.

November 16
International Day for Tolerance-

The Bible passage I chose for today is
Romans 14:1-10. Please, look it up and read it aloud
to the group.

Discuss how this Bible passage relates to today's
holiday.

Activity Suggestions:
1) This is a good day to learn about a different
culture (not religion). Listen to some (appropriate)
music from that country.
2) Listen to someone from a different political
party, and consider what they have to say. That
does not mean you will change your mind, but
maybe you will no longer see them as an evil
enemy.

What did you do today to observe this holiday?
Add any thoughts about your experience.

November 17
Electronic Greeting Card Day-

The Bible passage I chose for today is
Romans 12:10. Please, look it up and read it aloud
to the group.

Discuss how this Bible passage relates to today's
holiday.

Activity Suggestion:
1) Send an e-card to someone you haven't spoken
to in awhile.

What did you do today to observe this holiday?
Add any thoughts about your experience.

November 18
National Epilepsy Awareness Month-

The Bible passage I chose for today is 3 John 1:2.
Please, look it up and read it aloud to the group.

Discuss how this Bible passage relates to today's
holiday.

Activity Suggestions:
1) Learn about epilepsy, and how to be of the most
support to someone who has epilepsy.
2) If you have epilepsy, get the help you need and
do what you need to do to take care of yourself.
3) Never make fun of anyone having a seizure or
any medical condition. Don't make fun of anyone
at all.

What did you do today to observe this holiday?
Add any thoughts about your experience.

November 19
World Philosophy Day-

The Bible passage I chose for today is James 1:5.
Please, look it up and read it aloud to the group.

Discuss how this Bible passage relates to today's
holiday.

Activity Suggestions:
1) Take the opportunity to think about some
important subjects, and think about why you
believe the way you do.
2) Ask your family members and friends their
thoughts on a few of these subjects. Listen and
think about their viewpoint. You can calmly discuss
after you have fully listened, but don't argue.

What did you do today to observe this holiday?
Add any thoughts about your experience.

November 20
Beautiful Day-

The Bible passage I chose for today is James 1:17.
Please, look it up and read it aloud to the group.

Discuss how this Bible passage relates to today's
holiday.

Activity Suggestions:
1) Spend some time outside enjoying the beauty of
God's creation.
2) Notice and appreciate all the wonderful little
things that happen throughout the day.

What did you do today to observe this holiday?
Add any thoughts about your experience.

November 21
World Hello Day-

The Bible passage I chose for today is
Matthew 5:47. Please, look it up and read it aloud to
the group.

Discuss how this Bible passage relates to today's
holiday.

Activity Suggestion:
1) Greet everyone you meet today. You never know
what someone is going through, and your smile and
greeting could make a positive difference in their
day.

What did you do today to observe this holiday?
Add any thoughts about your experience.

November 22
Prematurity Awareness Month-

The Bible passage I chose for today is
Psalm 127:3. Please, look it up and read it aloud to
the group.

Discuss how this Bible passage relates to today's
holiday.

Activity Suggestion:
1) Raise awareness and support to prevent
premature births, and to also help those who are
born prematurely.

What did you do today to observe this holiday?
Add any thoughts about your experience.

November 23
International Games Week-

The Bible passage I chose for today is
2 Timothy 2:5. Please, look it up and read it aloud
to the group.

Discuss how this Bible passage relates to today's
holiday.

Activity Suggestion:
1) Play a game together as a group. Remember that
good sportsmanship is more important than
winning.

What did you do today to observe this holiday?
Add any thoughts about your experience.

November 24
Celebrate Your Unique Talent Day-

The Bible passage I chose for today is
Romans 12:6-8. Please, look it up and read it aloud
to the group.

Discuss how this Bible passage relates to today's
holiday.

Activity Suggestions:
1) What interesting thing can you do? Enjoy it
today, and encourage others to show their unique
talents, also.
2) If you have always had an interest in trying a
unique skill or activity, try it today.

What did you do today to observe this holiday?
Add any thoughts about your experience.

November 25
International Day for the Elimination of
Violence against Women-

The Bible passage I chose for today is
Romans 13:10. Please, look it up and read it aloud
to the group.

Discuss how this Bible passage relates to today's
holiday.

Activity Suggestion:
1) Are you unintentionally encouraging violence
against women? Pay attention to the shows you
watch, the music you listen to, the jokes you laugh
at, and the social media you like or share. Do not
watch, listen to, or otherwise support anything that
you (and more importantly, God) don't really
approve of.

What did you do today to observe this holiday?
Add any thoughts about your experience.

November 26
National Long-Term Care Awareness Month-

The Bible passage I chose for today is
Matthew 25:35-36. Please, look it up and read it
aloud to the group.

Discuss how this Bible passage relates to today's
holiday.

Activity Suggestions:
1) Spend some time with someone in a long-term
care facility or who is homebound due to a chronic
illness.
2) If you cannot visit in person, video call them, call
them, or write to them.

What did you do today to observe this holiday?
Add any thoughts about your experience.

November 27
National Healthy Skin Month-

The Bible passage I chose for today is 3 John 1:2.
Please, look it up and read it aloud to the group.

Discuss how this Bible passage relates to today's
holiday.

Activity Suggestion:
1) Learn some tips to take care of your skin.
Incorporate as many as you can into your daily
routine.

What did you do today to observe this holiday?
Add any thoughts about your experience.

November 28
It's Letter Writing Day-

The Bible passage I chose for today is
Romans 12:10-13. Please, look it up and read it
aloud to the group.

Discuss how this Bible passage relates to today's
holiday.

Activity Suggestion:
1) Write a letter to someone who has not heard
from you in awhile.

What did you do today to observe this holiday?
Add any thoughts about your experience.

November 29
Electronic Greeting Day-

The Bible passage I chose for today is
Romans 13:8. Please, look it up and read it aloud to
the group.

Discuss how this Bible passage relates to today's
holiday.

Activity Suggestion:
1) Send someone an unexpected email or text to let
them know you are thinking of them.

What did you do today to observe this holiday?
Add any thoughts about your experience.

November 30
National Inspirational Role Models Month-

The Bible passage I chose for today is Titus 2:7-8.
Please, look it up and read it aloud to the group.

Discuss how this Bible passage relates to today's
holiday.

Activity Suggestions:
1) Let someone know the positive influence they
have had on your life.
2) Do your best to be a good role model for those
who look up to you.

What did you do today to observe this holiday?
Add any thoughts about your experience.

13
DECEMBER

December 1
World AIDS Day-

The Bible passage I chose for today is 3 John 1:2.
Please, look it up and read it aloud to the group.

Discuss how this Bible passage relates to today's holiday.

Activity Suggestions:
1) Learn about AIDS prevention.
2) If you have AIDS, do what you need to do to take care of yourself and keep others safe.
3) Learn how to help those with the disease, and always be kind.

What did you do today to observe this holiday?
Add any thoughts about your experience.

December 2
Special Education Day-

The Bible passage I chose for today is
Matthew 7:12. Please, look it up and read it aloud to
the group.

Discuss how this Bible passage relates to today's
holiday.

Activity Suggestions:
1) Learn about the different reasons that students
receive special education classes.
2) Be kind and supportive to those students and
their teachers.
3) Do not exclude people because their strengths
and challenges are different than yours.

What did you do today to observe this holiday?
Add any thoughts about your experience.

December 3
International Day of Persons with Disabilities-

The Bible passage I chose for today is
Romans 12:10. Please, look it up and read it aloud
to the group.

Discuss how this Bible passage relates to today's
holiday.

Activity Suggestion:
1) Be sure to greet people who have a disability. Do
not overlook or ignore them.

What did you do today to observe this holiday?
Add any thoughts about your experience.

December 4
World Wildlife Conservation Day-

The Bible passage I chose for today is
Psalm 50:10-11. Please, look it up and read it aloud
to the group.

Discuss how this Bible passage relates to today's
holiday.

Activity Suggestions:
1) Learn about endangered animals.
2) Learn about wildlife in any habitat you choose.
3) Watch a video about wildlife in any habitat you
choose.

What did you do today to observe this holiday?
Add any thoughts about your experience.

December 5
International Volunteer Day for Economic &
Social Development-

The Bible passage I chose for today is
Mark 10:43-45. Please, look it up and read it aloud
to the group.

Discuss how this Bible passage relates to today's
holiday.

Activity Suggestions:
1) Volunteer at a local agency.
2) Help someone in need.
3) Put on some gloves; grab a garbage bag; and take
a walk through your local park or around your
neighborhood to pick up the trash along the way.
Take any and all precautions to stay safe. Call the
proper authorities to remove anything hazardous.

What did you do today to observe this holiday?
Add any thoughts about your experience.

December 6
St. Nicholas Day-

The Bible passage I chose for today is 1 John 3:17. Please, look it up and read it aloud to the group.

Note: It seems that Martin Luther, during the Protestant reformation, wanted to continue the tradition of giving toys to children, but wanted to move it from Saint Nicholas' Day to Christmas, so the focus would be on Jesus and not a saint (Henry, 2020). However, it seems to have back-fired, and Santa Claus became a huge part of Christmas anyway, commercialism took over, and it overshadows Jesus. Christian holidays should not be intermingled with those of other religions (religious syncretism), and as I've stated earlier, celebrating His birthday on December 25th is sharing His birthday with the supposed sun god's birthday (Geller, 2016), and nowhere near when most scholars believe He was actually born (Castro & Leggett, 2021). (I encourage you to do your own investigating into these matters, if you wish). I think it best to separate them again. We are not worshipping the saint, just respecting his memory. I think it best to keep the gift giving with St. Nicholas (although not as elaborate or commercialized as what is happening now with Christmas), celebrate Jesus' birthday without commercialism in July, and keep it all away from December 25.

Discuss how this Bible passage relates to today's holiday.

Activity Suggestion:
1) Learn about the life of St. Nicholas.

What did you do today to observe this holiday?
Add any thoughts about your experience.

December 7
Spiritual Literacy Month-

The Bible passage I chose for today is
Joshua 1:8. Please, look it up and read it aloud to
the group.

Discuss how this Bible passage relates to today's
holiday.

Activity Suggestions:
1) Memorize the order of the books of the Bible, so
you can more easily find the passages that you are
looking for.
2) Learn how the Bible is organized, and what is in
each section.
3) Memorize the 10 Commandments.
4) Buy, print, or make a poster of the 10
Commandments and hang it on the wall of your
home or post on your refrigerator.

What did you do today to observe this holiday?
Add any thoughts about your experience.

December 8
National Impaired Driving Prevention Month-

The Bible passage I chose for today is Galatians 6:1.
Please, look it up and read it aloud to the group.

Discuss how this Bible passage relates to today's
holiday.

Activity Suggestions:
1) Do not drink and drive or drive while intoxicated
on any substance.
2) Offer a ride home, or call a cab, for someone
who is intoxicated or otherwise not fit to drive.
3) Do not text and drive.
4) Learn what you can about how substances and
texting impair driving.

What did you do today to observe this holiday?
Add any thoughts about your experience.

December 9
International Anti-Corruption Day-

The Bible passage I chose for today is
Proverbs 20:10-11. Please, look it up and read it
aloud to the group.

Discuss how this Bible passage relates to today's
holiday.

Activity Suggestions:
1) Make a point to be honest in all of your words
and actions
2) Encourage others to be honest. Do not cover for
the sins of others.

What did you do today to observe this holiday?
Add any thoughts about your experience.

December 10
Dewey Decimal System Day-

The Bible passage I chose for today is
Proverbs 18:15. Please, look it up and read it aloud
to the group.

Discuss how this Bible passage relates to today's
holiday.

Activity Suggestions:
1) Learn about the Dewey Decimal System and
how to use it to find the type of book you want.
2) Visit a library and select a book to read. Take
someone with you, if you can.

What did you do today to observe this holiday?
Add any thoughts about your experience.

December 11
Write to a Friend Month-

The Bible passage I chose for today is
Acts 10:34-35. Please, look it up and read it aloud
to the group.

Discuss how this Bible passage relates to today's
holiday.

Activity Suggestion:
1) Write a kind letter to someone who may feel
lonely or depressed, or otherwise would really
appreciate someone reaching out to them.

What did you do today to observe this holiday?
Add any thoughts about your experience.

December 12
National 12-Hour Fresh Breath Day-

The Bible passage I chose for today is 3 John 1:2.
Please, look it up and read it aloud to the group.

Discuss how this Bible passage relates to today's
holiday.

Activity Suggestions:
1) Learn about and maintain good oral hygiene
habits.

What did you do today to observe this holiday?
Add any thoughts about your experience.

December 13
National Violin Day-

The Bible passage I chose for today is
Psalm 98:4-6. Please, look it up and read it aloud to
the group.

Discuss how this Bible passage relates to today's
holiday.

Activity Suggestion:
1) Listen to some violin music today.

What did you do today to observe this holiday?
Add any thoughts about your experience.

December 14
Yoga Day-

The Bible passage I chose for today is
Proverbs 31:17. Please, look it up and read it aloud
to the group.

Discuss how this Bible passage relates to today's
holiday.

Activity Suggestion:
1) Practice yoga together as a group. You can find
videos online to use.

What did you do today to observe this holiday?
Add any thoughts about your experience.

December 15
Bill of Rights Day-

The Bible passage I chose for today is
Romans 13:7-10. Please, look it up and read it aloud
to the group.

*Note: This passage was chosen to help balance rights and
responsibilities.*

Discuss how this Bible passage relates to today's
holiday.

Activity Suggestion:
1) Read the Bill of Rights for yourself.

What did you do today to observe this holiday?
Add any thoughts about your experience.

December 16
Boston Tea Party Day-

The Bible passage I chose for today is
Proverbs 18:15. Please, look it up and read it aloud
to the group.

Discuss how this Bible passage relates to today's
holiday.

Activity Suggestion:
1) Learn about the Boston Tea Party. Try to learn
more than you remember from your school days.

What did you do today to observe this holiday?
Add any thoughts about your experience.

December 17
Take a New Year's Resolution to Stop Smoking
(Dec 17th- Feb 5th)-

The Bible passage I chose for today is
1 Corinthians 6:20. Please, look it up and read it
aloud to the group.

Discuss how this Bible passage relates to today's
holiday.

Activity Suggestions:
1) Determine your reasons to quit; gather up your
support system; and set your quit date.
2) If you know someone who smokes, offer to be a
support system for him/her.

What did you do today to observe this holiday?
Add any thoughts about your experience.

December 18
Human Rights Month-

The Bible passage I chose for today is Job 34:19.
Please, look it up and read it aloud to the group.

Discuss how this Bible passage relates to today's
holiday.

Activity Suggestions:
1) Make an effort to greet those you may normally
walk past.
2) Treat everyone with dignity, no matter their
position in life.

What did you do today to observe this holiday?
Add any thoughts about your experience.

December 19
International Migrants Day-

The Bible passage I chose for today is Exodus 23:9.
Please, look it up and read it aloud to the group.

Discuss how this Bible passage relates to today's
holiday.

Activity Suggestions:
1) Learn your family's history. What countries were
your ancestor's from? When did they come to this
country?
2) Go out of your way to be kind to someone who
recently came to the United States.

What did you do today to observe this holiday?
Add any thoughts about your experience.

December 20
World Day of Prayer and Action for Children-

The Bible passage I chose for today is
1 Thessalonians 5:17. Please, look it up and read it
aloud to the group.

Discuss how this Bible passage relates to today's
holiday.

Activity Suggestion:
1) Pray for all of the children of the world.

What did you do today to observe this holiday?
Add any thoughts about your experience.

December 21
Crossword Puzzle Day-

The Bible passage I chose for today is
Proverbs 18:15. Please, look it up and read it aloud
to the group.

Discuss how this Bible passage relates to today's
holiday.

Activity Suggestion:
1) Complete a crossword puzzle today. You may
want to work on one alone, or work together as a
group.

What did you do today to observe this holiday?
Add any thoughts about your experience.

December 22
National Haiku Poetry Day-

The Bible passage I chose for today is
Philippians 4:8. Please, look it up and read it aloud
to the group.

Discuss how this Bible passage relates to today's
holiday.

Activity Suggestion:
1) Learn about Haiku poetry, and then write a
poem in that style.

What did you do today to observe this holiday?
Add any thoughts about your experience.

December 23
Look on the Bright Side Day-

The Bible passage I chose for today is
Colossians 3:15. Please, look it up and read it aloud
to the group.

Discuss how this Bible passage relates to today's
holiday.

Activity Suggestion:
1) Guard and guide your thoughts and attitudes to
see the positive in whatever you can.

What did you do today to observe this holiday?
Add any thoughts about your experience.

December 24
Worldwide Food Service Safety Day-

The Bible passage I chose for today is 3 John 1:2.
Please, look it up and read it aloud to the group.

Discuss how this Bible passage relates to today's
holiday.

Activity Suggestion:
1) Learn about safe food handling and storing
practices. These things are important for all of us to
know.

What did you do today to observe this holiday?
Add any thoughts about your experience.

December 25
It's About Time Week (Dec 25ᵗʰ- 31ˢᵗ)-

The Bible passage I chose for today is
Ephesians 5:15-17. Please, look it up and read it
aloud to the group.

Discuss how this Bible passage relates to today's
holiday.

Activity Suggestion:
1) Today is the day to do whatever you've been
putting off. Have you called your mom, dad,
grandma, or grandpa lately? Do it today. Do you
need to forgive someone? Today's your day.

What did you do today to observe this holiday?
Add any thoughts about your experience.

December 26
National Thank-You Note Day/National Whiner's Day-

The Bible passage I chose for today is
1 Corinthians 1:4. Please, look it up and read it
aloud to the group.

Discuss how this Bible passage relates to today's
holiday.

Activity Suggestion:
1) Combine these holidays. Instead of whining,
write thank you notes to people who have been a
blessing in your life.

What did you do today to observe this holiday?
Add any thoughts about your experience.

December 27
Make Cut-Out Snowflakes Day-

The Bible passage I chose for today is Job 37:6.
Please, look it up and read it aloud to the group.

Discuss how this Bible passage relates to today's
holiday.

Activity Suggestion:
1) Make cut-out snowflakes yourself or with your
children. You may use them for cards or
decorations.

What did you do today to observe this holiday?
Add any thoughts about your experience.

December 28
Call a Friend Day-

The Bible passage I chose for today is
1 Thessalonians 5:11. Please, look it up and read it
aloud to the group.

Discuss how this Bible passage relates to today's
holiday.

Activity Suggestion:
1) Spend some time today thinking about
friendship- who God would consider a good friend,
and how to be a good friend. Then, call a friend
today.

What did you do today to observe this holiday?
Add any thoughts about your experience.

December 29
Tick Tock Day-

The Bible passage I chose for today is Galatians 6:2.
Please, look it up and read it aloud to the group.

Discuss how this Bible passage relates to today's
holiday.

Activity Suggestion:
1) Find someone who is stressed and over-busy,
and offer to do something to reduce their burden.

What did you do today to observe this holiday?
Add any thoughts about your experience.

December 30
No Interruptions Day (last business day of the year)-

The Bible passage I chose for today is
Matthew 6:31-33. Please, look it up and read it
aloud to the group.

Discuss how this Bible passage relates to today's
holiday.

Activity Suggestion:
1) Instead of using this for business, use this for
your spouse, child, or family time. Set aside some
time where you only answer your phone for an
emergency, and have some uninterrupted quality
time.

What did you do today to observe this holiday?
Add any thoughts about your experience.

December 31
World Peace Meditation Day-

The Bible passage I chose for today is
Romans 12:18. Please, look it up and read it aloud
to the group.

Discuss how this Bible passage relates to today's
holiday.

Activity Suggestion:
1) Make a true effort to make peace today with
someone you have a grudge against, or who has a
grudge against you.

What did you do today to observe this holiday?
Add any thoughts about your experience.

14
REFLECTION

Come to this chapter once you have completed the entire book. If you started anywhere other than the beginning, circle back around until you have completed an entire year.

Now is the time to reflect on your journey.

What were some struggles you encountered on your journey?

Have you noticed any positive changes in yourself since you first began this journey? What are they?

Have you noticed any positive changes in your relationships with others? List them here.

How will you continue your journey?

Bibliography

Castro, J., & Leggett, J. (2021, November 19). *When Was Jesus Born?* Retrieved from Live Science: https://www.livescience.com/42976-when-was-jesus-born.html

Gellar, P. (2016, October 26). *Sol Invictus.* Retrieved from Mythology.net: https://mythology.net/roman/roman-gods/sol-invictus/

Henry, Fr. M. (2020, December 31). *Would Christmas be Christmas without Martin Luther?* Retrieved from St. Nicholas Center: https://www.stnicholascenter.org/who-is-st-nicholas/origin-of-santa/reformation-st-nicholas/christmas-martin-luther#:~:text=As%20the%20Reformation%20took%20hold%20over%20large%20swathes,Christ-child%2C%20rather%20than%20St%20Nicholas%2C%20the%20ultimate%2

MAY GOD CONTINUE TO BLESS
YOU ON YOUR JOURNEY

Made in the USA
Middletown, DE
27 March 2022